SOFTWARE ENGINEERING

SE

RAHUL SHARMA

Copyright © Rahul Sharma
All Rights Reserved.

This book has been published with all efforts taken to make the material error-free after the consent of the author. However, the author and the publisher do not assume and hereby disclaim any liability to any party for any loss, damage, or disruption caused by errors or omissions, whether such errors or omissions result from negligence, accident, or any other cause.

While every effort has been made to avoid any mistake or omission, this publication is being sold on the condition and understanding that neither the author nor the publishers or printers would be liable in any manner to any person by reason of any mistake or omission in this publication or for any action taken or omitted to be taken or advice rendered or accepted on the basis of this work. For any defect in printing or binding the publishers will be liable only to replace the defective copy by another copy of this work then available.

This book is dedicated to my late mentor and my friends who taught me the discipline of being a responsible person. The book is also dedicated to my students — past, present, and future. You are the object of my inspiration and motivation; you are the reason for this book.

Contents

Preface

The aim of this textbook The goal of this textbook is to introduce concepts of object-oriented software development and the programming language Smalltalk as a vehicle for their implementation.

Acknowledgements

I would like to thank to my teachers who supported me all the time, cleared my doubts and to my parents who also played a big role in finalization of my book. I am taking this opportunity to acknowledge their support and I wish that they keep supporting me like this in the future.

CHAPTER ONE

Introduction to Software and Software Engineering

(1) Software & Software Engineering

Software:

- Computer software is the product that software professionals build and then support over the long term.
- It encompasses programs that execute within a computer of any size and architecture, content that is presented as the computer programs execute, and descriptive information in both hard copy and virtual forms that encompass virtually any electronic media.

Characteristics of software:

1. Software is developed or engineered; it is not manufactured in the classical sense:

- Although some similarities exist between software development and hardware manufacturing, but few activities are fundamentally different.
- In both activities, high quality is achieved through good design, but the manufacturing phase for hardware can introduce quality problems than software.

1. Software doesn't "wear out."

- Hardware components suffer from the growing effects of dust, vibration, abuse, temperature extremes, and many other environmental maladies. Stated simply, the hardware begins to wear out.
- Software is not susceptible to the environmental maladies that cause hardware to wear out. In theory, therefore, the failure rate curve for software should take the form of the "idealized curve".
- When a hardware component wears out, it is replaced by a spare part.
- There are no software spare parts.
- Every software failure indicates an error in design or in the process through which design was translated into machine executable code.
- Therefore, the software maintenance tasks that accommodate requests for change involve considerably more complexity than hardware maintenance.

However, the implication is clear—software doesn't wear out. But it does deteriorate.

Hardware Failure curve Software Failure curve

1. Although the industry is moving toward component-based construction, most software continues to be custom built.

- A software component should be designed and implemented so that it can be reused in many different programs.
- Modern reusable components encapsulate both data and the processing that is applied to the data, enabling the software engineer to create new applications from reusable parts.
- In the hardware world, component reuse is a natural part of the engineering process
-

Difference between program and software

Program Software

1. Small in size.
2. Authors himself is user-soul.
3. Single developer.
4. Adopt development.
5. Lack proper interface.
6. Large proper documentation.

-

Software Myths:

- Large in size.
- Large number.
- Team developer.
- Systematic development.
- Well define interface.

- Well documented
- Software myths are beliefs about software and the process used to build it.
- Management Myths:
- Myth 1:

We already have a book that's full of standards and procedures for building software. Won't that provide my people with everything they need to know?

Reality:

- The book of standards may very well exist, but is it used?
- Are software practitioners aware of its existence?
- Does it reflect modern software engineering practice? Is it complete? Is it adaptable?
- Is it streamlined to improve time-to-delivery while still maintaining a focus on quality?
- In many cases, the answer to all of these questions is no.

- Myth 2:

If we get behind schedule, we can add more programmers and catch up.

Reality:

- Software development is not a mechanistic process like manufacturing.
- As new people are added, people who were working must spend time educating the newcomers, thereby reducing the amount of time spent on productive development effort.
- People can be added but only in a planned and well-coordinated manner.

- Myth 3:

  If I decide to outsource the software project to a third party, I can just relax and let that firm build it.

  Reality:

  - If an organization does not understand how to manage and control software projects internally, it will invariably struggle when it outsources software
- projects.

- Customer Myths:
- Myth 1:

  A general statement of objectives is sufficient to begin writing programs—we can fill in the details later.

  Reality:

  - Although a comprehensive and stable statement of requirements is not always possible, an ambiguous "statement of objectives" is a recipe for disaster.
  - Unambiguous requirements are developed only through effective and continuous communication between customer and developer.

- Myth 2:

  Software requirements continually change, but change can be easily accommodated because software is flexible.

  Reality:

  - It is true that software requirements change, but the impact of change varies with the time at which it is introduced.
  - When requirements changes are requested early the cost impact is relatively small.

- However, as time passes, the cost impact grows rapidly—resources have been committed, a design framework has been established, and change can cause upheaval that requires additional resources and major design modification.

- Practitioner's Myths:
- Myth 1:

  Once we write the program and get it to work, our job is done.

  Reality:

  - Industry data indicate that between 60 and 80 percent of all effort expended on software will be expended after it is delivered to the customer for the first time.

- Myth 2:

  Until I get the program "running" I have no way of assessing its quality.

  Reality:

  - One of the most effective software quality assurance mechanisms can be applied from the inception of a project—the technical review.
  - Software reviews are a "quality filter" that have been found to be more effective than testing for finding certain classes of software defects.

- Myth 3:

  The only deliverable work product for a successful project is the working program.

Reality:

- A working program is only one part of a software configuration that includes many elements.
- A variety of work products (e.g., models, documents, plans) provide a foundation for successful engineering and, more important, guidance for software support.

- Myth 4:
Software engineering will make us create voluminous and unnecessary documentation and will invariably slow us down.
Reality:

- Software engineering is not about creating documents.
- It is about creating a quality product.
- Better quality leads to reduced rework.
- And reduced rework results in faster delivery times.

-

Software Engineering:

- Software Engineering is the application of a systematic, disciplined, quantifiable approach to the development, operation, and maintenance of software; that is, the application of engineering to software.

-

A Layered Technology:

A quality Focus:

<u>Figure: Software Engineering Layers</u>

- Every organization is rest on its **commitment to quality.**
- Total **quality management, Six Sigma, or similar continuous improvement culture** and it is this culture ultimately leads to development of increasingly more effective approaches to software engineering.
- The foundation that supports software engineering is a quality focus.
- ***Process:***
- The software engineering process is the glue that holds the technology layers together and enables rational and timely development of computer software.
- Process defines a framework that must be established for effective delivery of software engineering technology.
- The software process forms the basis for management control of software projects and establishes the context in which technical methods are applied, work products are produced, milestones are established, quality is ensured, and change is properly managed.
- ***Methods:***

- Software engineering methods provide the technical aspects for building software.
- Methods encompass a broad array of tasks that include communication, requirements analysis, design modeling, program construction, testing, and support.
- Software engineering methods rely on the set of modeling activities and other descriptive techniques.
- ***Tools:***
- Software engineering tools provide automated or semi-automated support for the process and the methods.
- When tools are integrated so that information created by one tool can be used by another, a system for the support of software development, called **CASE** (computer-aided software engineering), is established.
- Process & Generic Process Model
- A software process is defined as a collection of work activities, actions, and tasks that are performed when some work product is to be created.
- Each of these activities, actions, and tasks reside within a framework or model that defines their relationship with the process and with one another.

Figure: Generic Process Model

- Each framework activity is populated by a set of software engineering actions.
- Each software engineering action is defined by a task set that identifies the work tasks that are to be completed, the work products that will be produced, the quality assurance points that will be required, and the milestones that will be used to indicate progress.
- A generic process framework for software engineering defines **five framework activities— communication, planning, modeling, construction, and deployment**.
- In addition, it defines a set of umbrella activities.
-

Process Flow:

- **Process flow**—describes how the framework activities and the actions and tasks that occur within each framework activity are organized with respect to sequence and time.

- A linear process flow executes each of the five framework activities in sequence, beginning with communication and culminating with deployment.
- An iterative process flow repeats one or more of the activities before proceeding to the next.
- An evolutionary process flow executes the activities in a "circular" manner. Each circuit through the five activities leads to a more complete version of the software.
- A parallel process flow executes one or more activities
- in parallel with other activities.
- Umbrella Activities
- Software engineering process framework activities are complemented by a number of umbrella activities.
- In general, umbrella activities are applied throughout a software project and help a software team manage and control progress, quality, change, and risk.
- Typical umbrella activities include:

    Software project tracking and control—allows the software team to assess progress against the project plan and take any necessary action to maintain the schedule.

    Risk management—assesses risks that may affect the outcome of the project or the quality of the product.

    Software quality assurance—defines and conducts the activities required to ensure software quality.

    Technical reviews—assesses software engineering work products in an effort to uncover and remove errors before they are propagated to the next activity.

    Measurement—defines and collects process, project, and product measures that assist the team in delivering software that meets stakeholders' needs; can be used in conjunction with all other framework and umbrella activities.

Software configuration management—manages the effects of change throughout the software process.

Reusability management—defines criteria for work product reuse (including software components) and establishes mechanisms to achieve reusable components.

Work product preparation and production—encompasses the activities required to create work products such as models, documents, logs, forms, and lists.

- Prescriptive Process Models
- Prescriptive process models were originally proposed to bring order to the chaos of software development.
- Traditional models have brought a certain amount of useful structure to software engineering work and have provided a reasonably effective road map for software teams.
- Following are prescriptive process models:
- –Waterfall model
    –Incremental Model

    - RAD Model

- –Evolutionary Process Model

    - Prototype Model
    - Spiral Model
  - Concurrent Process Model

- Waterfall Process Model
- The waterfall model, sometimes called the classic life cycle, suggests a systematic, sequential approach to

software development that begins with customer specification of requirements and progresses through planning, modeling, construction, and deployment, culminating in ongoing support of the completed software.

Limitations:

Figure: Waterfall Model

- The nature of the requirements will not change very much during development; during evolution.
- The model implies that you should attempt to complete a given stage before moving on to the next stage.
- Does not account for the fact that requirements constantly change.
- It also means that customers cannot use anything until the entire system is complete.
- The model implies that once the product is finished, everything else is maintenance.
- Surprises at the end are very expensive
- Some teams sit ideal for other teams to finish
- Therefore, this model is only appropriate when the requirements are well-understood and changes will be fairly limited during the design process.
-

When to use waterfall model?

- Requirements are very well known, clear and fixed
- Product definition is stable
- Technology is understood
- There are no ambiguous requirements
- Ample resources with required expertise are available freely
- The project is short
- Incremental Process Model
- The incremental model combines elements of linear and parallel process flows.
- The incremental model applies linear sequences in a staggered fashion as calendar time progresses.
- Each linear sequence produces deliverable "increments" of the software.

-

For example, word-processing software developed using the incremental paradigm might deliver basic file management, editing, and document production functions in the first increment; more sophisticated editing and document production capabilities in the second increment; spelling and grammar checking in the third increment; and advanced page layout capability in the fourth increment.

*

Advantages:

Figure: Incremental Process Model
- Generates working software quickly and early during the software life cycle.
- This model is more flexible – less costly to change scope and requirements.
- It is easier to test and debug during a smaller iteration.
- In this model customer can respond to each built.
- Lowers initial delivery cost.
- Easier to manage risk because risky pieces are identified and handled during iteration.

*

Disadvantages:

- Needs good planning and design.
- Needs a clear and complete definition of the whole system before it can be broken down and built incrementally.
- Total cost is higher than waterfall.

*

When to use waterfall model?

- This model can be used when the requirements of the complete system are clearly defined and understood.
- Major requirements must be defined; however, some details can evolve with time.

- There is a need to get a product to the market early.
- A new technology is being used.
- Resources with needed skill set are not available.
- There are some high risk features and goals.

1. RAD (Rapid Application Development) Process Model

- It is a type of incremental model. In RAD model the components or functions are developed in parallel as if they were mini projects.
- The developments are time boxed, delivered and then assembled into a working prototype.
- This can quickly give the customer something to see and use and to provide feedback regarding the delivery and their requirements.

Figure: Rapid Application Development Model

Advantages:

- Reduced development time.
- Increases reusability of components
- Quick initial reviews occur
- Encourages customer feedback
- Integration from very beginning solves a lot of integration issues.

Disadvantages:

- For large but scalable projects RAD requires sufficient human resources.
- Projects fail if developers and customers are not committed in a much shortened time-frame.
- Problematic if system cannot be modularized.
- Not appropriate when technical risks are high (heavy use of new technology).

When to use RAD model?

- RAD should be used when there is a need to create a system that can be modularized in 2-3 months of time.
- It should be used if there's high availability of designers for modeling and the budget is high enough to afford their cost along with the cost of automated code generating tools.
- RAD SDLC model should be chosen only if resources with high business knowledge are available and there is a need to produce the system in a short span of time (2-3 months).

3. Prototype process model

- The basic idea here is that instead of freezing the requirements before a design or coding can proceed, a throwaway prototype is built to understand the requirements.

- This prototype is developed based on the currently known requirements.
- By using this prototype, the client can get an "actual feel" of the system, since the interactions with prototype can enable the client to better understand the requirements of the desired system.
- Prototyping is an attractive idea for complicated and large systems for which there is no manual process or existing system to help determining the requirements.
- The prototype are usually not complete systems and many of the details are not built in the prototype. The goal is to provide a system with overall functionality.

Advantages:

Figure: Prototype Model

- Users are actively involved in the development
- Since in this methodology a working model of the system is provided, the users get a better understanding of the system being developed.
- Errors can be detected much earlier.
- Quicker user feedback is available leading to better solutions.
- Missing functionality can be identified easily
- Confusing or difficult functions can be identified

Disadvantages:

- Leads to implementing and then repairing way of building systems.
- Practically, this methodology may increase the complexity of the system as scope of the system may expand beyond original plans.
- Incomplete application may cause application not to be used as the full system was designed.

When to use Prototype Model?

- Prototype model should be used when the desired system needs to have a lot of interaction with the end users.
- Typically, online systems, web interfaces have a very high amount of interaction with end users, are best

suited for Prototype model. It might take a while for a system to be built that allows ease of use and needs minimal training for the end user.

- Prototyping ensures that the end users constantly work with the system and provide a feedback which is incorporated in the prototype to result in a useable system. They are excellent for designing good human computer interface systems.

4. Spiral process model

- It was originally proposed by Barry Boehm, the spiral model is an evolutionary software process model that couples the iterative nature of prototyping with the controlled and systematic aspects of the waterfall model.
- It provides the potential for rapid development of increasingly more complete versions of the software.
- The spiral development model is a risk-driven process model generator that is used to guide multi- stakeholder concurrent engineering of software intensive systems.
- It has two main distinguishing features. One is a cyclic approach for incrementally growing a system's degree of definition and implementation while decreasing its degree of risk.
- The other is a set of anchor point milestones for ensuring stakeholder commitment to feasible and mutually satisfactory system solutions.

Figure: Spiral Process Model

- The first circuit around the spiral might result in the development of a product specification; subsequent passes around the spiral might be used to develop a prototype and then progressively more sophisticated versions of the software.
- Each pass through the planning region results in adjustments to the project plan.
- Cost and schedule are adjusted based on feedback derived from the customer after delivery.
- In addition, the project manager adjusts the planned number of iterations required to complete the software.

Advantages:

- High amount of risk analysis hence, avoidance of Risk is enhanced.
- Good for large and mission-critical projects.
- Strong approval and documentation control.
- Additional Functionality can be added at a later date.
- Software is produced early in the software life cycle.

Disadvantages:

- Can be a costly model to use.
- Risk analysis requires highly specific expertise.
- Project's success is highly dependent on the risk analysis phase.
- Doesn't work well for smaller projects.

When to use spiral process model?

- When costs and risk evaluation is important for medium to high-risk projects.
- Long-term project commitment unwise because of potential changes to economic priorities
- Users are unsure of their needs.
- Requirements are complex
- New product line Significant changes are expected (research and exploration)

5. Concurrent Process Model

- The concurrent development model, sometimes called concurrent engineering, allows a software team to represent iterative and concurrent elements of any of the process models.
- For example, the modeling activity defined for the spiral model is accomplished by invoking one or more of the following software engineering actions: prototyping, analysis, and design.
- The activity—modeling—may be in any one of the states noted at any given time.
- Similarly, other activities, actions, or tasks (e.g., communication or construction) can be represented in an analogous manner.
- All software engineering activities exist concurrently but reside in different states.

Figure: Concurrent Process Model

6. Component Based Development

- Commercial off-the-shelf (COTS) software components, developed by vendors who offer them as products, provide targeted functionality with well-defined interfaces that enable the component to be integrated into the software that is to be built.

- The component-based development model incorporates many of the characteristics of the spiral model.
- It is evolutionary in nature, demanding an iterative approach to the creation of software.
- However, the component-based development model constructs applications from prepackaged software components.

The component-based development model incorporates the following steps:

1. Available component-based products are researched and evaluated for the application domain in question.
2. Component integration issues are considered.
3. A software architecture is designed to accommodate the components.
4. Components are integrated into the architecture.
5. Comprehensive testing is conducted to ensure proper functionality.

- The component-based development model leads to software reuse, and reusability provides software engineers with a number of measurable benefits.

7. Agile Process Model

- Agile SDLC model is a combination of iterative and incremental process models with focus on process adaptability and customer satisfaction by rapid delivery of working software product.
- Agile Methods break the product into small incremental builds.

- Every iteration involves cross functional teams working simultaneously on various areas like planning, requirements analysis, design, coding, unit testing, and acceptance testing.

Advantages:

- Customer satisfaction by rapid, continuous delivery of useful software.
- Customers, developers and testers constantly interact with each other.
- Close, daily cooperation between business people and developers.
- Continuous attention to technical excellence and good design.
- Regular adaptation to changing circumstances.
- Even late changes in requirements are welcomed

Disadvantages:

- In case of some software, it is difficult to assess the effort required at the beginning of the software development life cycle.
- There is lack of emphasis on necessary designing and documentation.
- The project can easily get taken off track if the customer representative is not clear what final outcome that they want.

- Only senior programmers are capable of taking the kind of decisions required during the development process.

8. Product and Process

- If the process is weak, the end product will undoubtedly suffer.
- But a compulsive overreliance on process is also dangerous.
- People derive as much (or more) satisfaction from the creative process as they do from the end product.
- An artist enjoys the brush strokes as much as the framed result.
- A writer enjoys the search for the proper metaphor as much as the finished book.
- As creative software professional, you should also derive as much satisfaction from the process as the end product.
- The duality of product and process is one important element in keeping creative people engaged as software engineering continues to evolve.

CHAPTER TWO

Agile Development

(1) Agility and Agile Process Model

Agility:

? Agility is dynamic, content specific, aggressively change embracing, and growth oriented

? It encourages team structures and attitudes that make communication (among team members, between technologists and business people, between software engineers and their managers) more simplistic.

? It emphasizes rapid delivery of operational software and de-emphasizes the importance of intermediate work products.

? It recognizes that planning in an uncertain world has its limits and that a project plan must be flexible.

? Agility can be applied to any software process.

Agile Process:

? Any agile software process is characterized in a manner that addresses a number of key assumptions

[1] It is difficult to predict in advance which software requirements will persist and which will change. It is equally difficult to predict how customer priorities will change as the project proceeds.

[2] For many types of software, design and construction are interleaved. That is, both activities should be performed

in tandem so that design models are proven as they are created. It is difficult to predict how much design is necessary before construction is used to prove the design.

[3] Analysis, design, construction, and testing are not as predictable as we might like.

Agility Principles:

1 Our highest priority is to satisfy the customer through early and continuous delivery of valuable software.

2 Welcome changing requirements, even late in development.

3 Deliver working software frequently, from a couple of weeks to a couple of months, with a preference to the shorter timescale.

4 Business people and developers must work together daily throughout the project.

5 Build projects around motivated individuals. Give them the environment and support they need, and trust them to get the job done.

6 The most efficient and effective method of conveying information to and within a development team is face-to-face conversation.

7 Working software is the primary measure of progress.

8 Agile processes promote sustainable development. The sponsors, developers, and users should be able to maintain a constant pace indefinitely.

9 Continuous attention to technical excellence and good design enhances agility.

10 Simplicity—the art of maximizing the amount of work not done—is essential.

11 The best architectures, requirements, and designs emerge from self– organizing teams.

12 At regular intervals, the team reflects on how to become more effective, then tunes and adjusts its behavior

accordingly.

Agile Process Models:

? Extreme Programming (XP)

? Adaptive Software Development (ASD)

? Dynamic Systems Development Method (DSDM)

? Scrum

? Crystal

? Feature Driven Development (FDD)

? Agile Modeling (AM)

1. Extreme Programming

- It is most widely used agile process model.
- XP uses an object-oriented approach as its preferred development paradigm.
- It defines four (4) framework activities **Planning, Design, Coding, and Testing.**

Planning:

Figure: Extreme Programming Process

- Begins with the creation of a set of stories (also called user stories)
- Each story is written by the customer and is placed on an index card
- The customer assigns a value (i.e. a priority) to the story
- Agile team assesses each story and assigns a cost
- Stories are grouped to for a deliverable increment
- A commitment is made on delivery date
- After the first increment "project velocity" is used to help define subsequent delivery dates for other increments

Design:

- Follows the keep it simple principle
- Encourage the use of CRC (class-responsibility-collaborator) cards
- For difficult design problems, suggests the creation of "spike solutions"—a design prototype
- Encourages "refactoring"—an iterative refinement of the internal program design
- Design occurs both before and after coding commences

Coding:

- Recommends the construction of a series of unit tests for each of the stories before coding commences
- Encourages "pair programming"

- Developers work in pairs, checking each other's work and providing the support to always do a good job.
- Mechanism for real-time problem solving and real-time quality assurance
- Keeps the developers focused on the problem at hand
- Needs continuous integration with other portions (stories) of the s/w, which provides a "smoke testing" environment

Testing:

- Unit tests should be implemented using a framework to make testing automated. This encourages a regression testing strategy.
- Integration and validation testing can occur on a daily basis
- Acceptance tests, also called customer tests, are specified by the customer and executed to assess customer visible functionality
- Acceptance tests are derived from user stories

Adaptive Software Development (ASD)

Adaptive Software Development (ASD) is a technique for building complex software and systems. ASD focus on human collaboration and team self-organization.

ASD incorporates three phases **Speculation, Collaboration, and Learning.**

Speculation:

Figure: Adaptive Software Development

- "Speculate" refers to the planning paradox—outcomes are unpredictable, therefore, endless suppositions on a product's look and feel are not likely to lead to any business value.
- The big idea behind speculate is when we plan a product to its smallest detail as in a requirements up front Waterfall variant, we produce the product we intend and not the product the customer needs.

- In the ASD mindset, planning is to speculation as intention is to need.

Collaboration:

- Collaboration represents a balance between managing the doing and creating and maintaining the collaborative environment.
- Speculation says we can't predict outcomes. If we can't predict outcomes, we can't plan. If we can't plan, traditional project management theory suffers.
- Collaboration weights speculation in that a project manager plans the work between the predictable parts of the environment and adapts to the uncertainties of various factors—stakeholders, requirements, software vendors, technology, etc.

Learning:

- "Learning" cycles challenge all stakeholders and project team members.
- Based on short iterations of design, build and testing, knowledge accumulates from the small mistakes we make due to false assumptions, poorly stated or ambiguous requirements or misunderstanding the stakeholders' needs.
- Correcting those mistakes through shared learning cycles leads to greater positive experience and eventual mastery of the problem domain.

Dynamic Systems Development Methods (DSDM)

- The Dynamic Systems Development Method is an agile software development approach that "provides a framework for building and maintaining systems which meet tight time constraints through the use of incremental prototyping in a controlled project environment"
- DSDM is an iterative software process in which each iteration follows the 80 percent rule.
- That is, only enough work is required for each increment to facilitate movement to the next increment.
- The remaining detail can be completed later when more business requirements are known or changes have been requested and accommodated.

DSDM life cycle that defines three different iterative cycles, preceded by two additional life cycle activities: **Feasibility study**—establishes the basic business requirements and constraints associated with the application to be built and then assesses whether the application is a viable candidate for the DSDM process. **Business study**—establishes the functional and information requirements that will allow the application to provide business value; also, defines the basic application architecture and identifies the maintainability requirements for the application.

Functional model iteration—produces a set of incremental prototypes that demonstrate functionality for the customer.

Design and build iteration—revisits prototypes built during functional model iteration to ensure that each has been engineered in a manner that will enable it to provide operational business value for end users.

Implementation—places the latest software increment into the operational environment.

- DSDM can be combined with XP to provide a combination approach that defines a solid process model (the DSDM life cycle) with the nuts and bolts practices (XP) that are required to build software increments.
- In addition, the ASD concepts of collaboration and self-organizing teams can be adapted to a combined process model.

Scrum

- Scrum principles are consistent with the agile manifesto and are used to guide development activities within a process that incorporates the five framework activities: **requirements, analysis, design, evolution, and delivery**.
- Within each framework activity, work tasks occur within a process pattern called a sprint.
- The work conducted within a sprint (the number of sprints required for each framework activity will vary depending on product complexity and size) is adapted to the problem at hand and is defined and often modified in real time by the Scrum team.

- Scrum emphasizes the use of a set of software process patterns that have proven effective for projects with tight timelines, changing requirements, and business criticality.
- Each of these process patterns defines a set of development actions: Backlog—a prioritized list of project requirements or features that provide business value for the customer.
- Items can be added to the backlog at any time (this is how changes are introduced).
- The product manager assesses the backlog and updates priorities as required.

Crystal

- The Crystal methodology is one of the most lightweight, adaptable approaches to software development. Crystal is actually comprised of a family of agile methodologies such as Crystal Clear, Crystal Yellow, Crystal Orange and others, whose unique characteristics are driven by several factors such as team size, system criticality, and project priorities.
- This Crystal family addresses the realization that each project may require a slightly tailored set of policies, practices, and processes in order to meet the project's unique characteristics.
- Several of the key tenets of Crystal include teamwork, communication, and simplicity, as well as reflection to frequently adjust and improve the process.
- Like other agile process methodologies, Crystal promotes early, frequent delivery of working software,

high user involvement, adaptability, and the removal of bureaucracy or distractions.

Feature Driven Development (FDD)

Figure: Feature Driven Development Model

- FDD is a model-driven, short-iteration process.
- It begins with establishing an overall model shape.
- Then it continues with a series of two-week "design by feature, build by feature" iterations.
- The features are small, "useful in the eyes of the client" results.
- FDD designs the rest of the development process around feature delivery using the following eight practices:

- Domain Object Modeling
- Developing by Feature
- Component/Class Ownership

- Feature Teams
- Inspections
- Configuration Management
- Regular Builds
- Visibility of progress and results
- FDD recommends specific programmer practices such as "Regular Builds" and "Component/Class Ownership".
- Unlike other agile methods, FDD describes specific, very short phases of work, which are to be accomplished separately per feature.
- These include Domain Walkthrough, Design, Design Inspection, Code, Code Inspection, and Promote to Build.

Agile Modeling (AM)

- Agile Modeling (AM) is a practice-based methodology for effective modeling and documentation of software-based systems.
- Simply put, Agile Modeling (AM) is a collection of values, principles, and practices for modeling software that can be applied on a software development project in an effective and light-weight manner.
- Although AM suggests a wide array of "core" and "supplementary" modeling principles, those that make AM unique are:

Use multiple models. There are many different models and notations that can be used to describe software. AM suggests that to provide needed insight, each model should present a different aspect of the system and only those models that provide value to their intended audience should be used.

Travel light. As software engineering work proceeds, keep only those models that will provide long-term value and jettison the rest.

Content is more important than representation. Modeling should impart information to its intended audience. A syntactically perfect model that imparts little useful content is not as valuable as a model with flawed notation that nevertheless provides valuable content for its audience.

Know the models and the tools you use to create them. Understand the strengths and weaknesses of each model and the tools that are used to create it.

Adapt locally. The modeling approach should be adapted to the needs of the agile team.

CHAPTER THREE

Managing Software Project

1. Software Metrics

Terminologies

- **Measure:** Quantitative indication of the extent, amount, dimension, or size of some attribute of a product or process.
- **Metrics:** The degree to which a system, component, or process possesses a given attribute. Relates several measures (e.g. average number of errors found per person hour)
- **Indicators:** A combination of metrics that provides insight into the software process, project or product
- **Direct Metrics:** Immediately measurable attributes (e.g. line of code, execution speed, defects reported)
- **Indirect Metrics:** Aspects that are not immediately quantifiable (e.g. functionality, quantity, reliability)
- Faults:

- **Errors:** Faults found by the practitioners during software development
- **Defects:** Faults found by the customers after release

Metric Classification

- Processes

  – Activities related to production of software

- Products

- Explicit results of software development activities.
- Deliverables, documentation, by products

- Project

- Inputs into the software development activities
- hardware, knowledge, people

Process Metrics

- Process metrics are collected across all projects and over long periods of time. Their intent is to provide a set of process indicators that lead to long-term software process improvement.
- Focus on quality achieved as a consequence of a repeatable or managed process.
- Strategic and Long Term.

- Statistical Software Process Improvement (SSPI). Error Categorization and Analysis:

- All errors and defects are categorized by origin
- The cost to correct each error and defect is recorded
- The number of errors and defects in each category is computed
- Data is analyzed to find categories that result in the highest cost to the organization
- Plans are developed to modify the process

Project Metrics

- Project metrics enable a software project manager to assess the status of an ongoing project, track potential risks, uncover problem areas before they go "critical," adjust work flow or tasks, and evaluate the project team's ability to control quality of software work products.
- Project metrics on most software projects occurs during estimation.
- Metrics collected from past projects are used as a basis from which effort and time estimates are made for current software work.

- Production rates represented in terms of models created, review hours, function points, and delivered source lines are measured.
- These metrics are used to minimize the development schedule by making the adjustments necessary to avoid delays and mitigate potential problems and risks.

- Project metrics are used to assess product quality on an ongoing basis and, when necessary, modify the technical approach to improve quality.

Product Metrics

- Focus on the quality of deliverables
- Product metrics are combined across several projects to produce process metrics
- Metrics for the product:

- Measures of the Analysis Model
- Complexity of the Design Model
- Internal algorithmic complexity
- Architectural complexity
- Data flow complexity
- Code metrics

1. Software Measurement

- Direct Measures (internal attributes)

  – Cost, effort, LOC, speed, memory

- Indirect Measures (external attributes)

  – Functionality, quality, complexity, efficiency, reliability, maintainability

Size Oriented metrics

- Size-oriented software metrics are derived by normalizing quality and/or productivity measures by considering the size of the software that has been produced.
  - simple size-oriented metrics for each project:

    - Errors per KLOC (thousand lines of code)
- Defects per KLOC
- $ per KLOC
- Pages of documentation per KLOC
- Errors per person-month
- KLOC per person-month
- $ per page of documentation

Function-Oriented metrics

- Function-oriented software metrics use a measure of the functionality delivered by the application as a normalization value.
- The most widely used function-oriented metric is the **function point (FP)**.
- Computation of the function point is based on characteristics of the software's information domain and complexity.

Object-Oriented Metrics

- Object-Oriented Metrics Conventional software project metrics (LOC or FP) can be used to estimate object-oriented software projects.

- However, these metrics do not provide enough granularity for the schedule and effort adjustments that are required as you iterate through an evolutionary or incremental process.

Use-Case–Oriented Metrics

- Like FP, the use case is defined early in the software process, allowing it to be used for estimation before significant modeling and construction activities are initiated.
- Use cases describe (indirectly, at least) user-visible functions and features that are basic requirements for a system. The use case is independent of programming language.
- Because use cases can be created at vastly different levels of abstraction, there is no standard "size" for a use case.
- Without a standard measure of what a use case is, its application as a normalization measure (e.g., effort expended per use case) is suspect.

3. Function Point Metrics

- Function point metrics provide a standardized method for measuring the various functions of a software application.
- Function point metrics, measure functionality from the user's point of view, that is, on the basis of what the user requests and receives in return.

Information domain values:

- Number of user inputs – Distinct input from user
- Number of user outputs – Reports, screens, error messages, etc.
- Number of user inquiries – On line input that generates some result
- Number of files – Logical file (database)
- Number of external interfaces – Data files/connections as interface to other systems Formula to count FP is

$FP = \text{Total Count} * [0.65 + 0.01*\sum(Fi)]$

Where, Total count is all the counts times a weighting factor that is determined for each organization via empirical data. Fi (i=1 to 14) are complexity adjustment values.

Value Adjustment Factors (Fi):

F1. Data Communication

F2. Distributed Data Processing

F3. Performance

F4. Heavily Used Configuration
F5. Transaction Role
F6. Online Data Entry
F7. End-User Efficiency
F8. Online Update
F9. Complex Processing
F10. Reusability
F13. Multiple Sites
F11. Installation Ease
F14. Facilitate Change
F12. Operational Ease
Example:
A simple example:
inputs
3 simple
X 3 = 9

4 average

X 4 = 16
1 complex
outputs
6 average
X 6 = 6
X 5 = 30
2 complex
files
5 complex
inquiries
8 average
interfaces
3 average
X 7 = 14
X 15 = 75
X 4 = 32

X 7 = 21

4 complex

X 10 = <u>40</u>

Unadjusted function points 243 F09. Complex internal processing

= 3

F10. Code to be reusable

= 2

F03. High performance

= 4

F13. Multiple sites

= 3

F02. Distributed processing

= <u>5</u>

Project adjustment factor

= 17

Adjustment calculation:

Adjusted FP = Unadjusted FP X [0.65 + (adjustment factor X 0.01)]

=

243

X [0.65 + (

17

X 0.01)]

=

243

X [0.82]

= 199.26 Adjusted function points

4. Software Project Estimation

- Software project estimation is a form of problem solving, and in most cases, the problem to be solved (i.e., developing a cost and effort estimate for a software project) is too complex to be considered in one piece.
- Estimation of resources, cost, and schedule for a software engineering effort requires experience, access to good historical information (metrics), and the courage to commit to quantitative predictions when qualitative information is all that exists.
- Software project estimation is a form of problem solving, and in most cases, the problem to be solved is too complex to be considered in one piece.
- For this reason, you should decompose the problem, characterizing it as a set of smaller (and hopefully, more manageable) problems.

Software Sizing

"Fuzzy logic" sizing:

- This approach uses the approximate reasoning techniques that are the cornerstone of fuzzy logic.
- To apply this approach, the planner must identify the type of application, establish its magnitude on a qualitative scale, and then refine the magnitude within the original range.

Function point sizing:

- The planner develops estimates of the information domain characteristics.

Standard component sizing:

- Software is composed of a number of different "standard components" that are generic to a particular application area.

Change sizing:

- This approach is used when a project encompasses the use of existing software that must be modified in some way as part of a project.
- The planner estimates the number and type (e.g., reuse, adding code, changing code, and deleting code) of modifications that must be accomplished.

Problem-Based Estimation

- Start with a bounded statement of scope
- Decompose the software into problem functions that can each be estimated individually
- Compute an LOC or FP value for each function
- Derive cost or effort estimates by applying the LOC or FP values to your baseline productivity metrics (e.g., LOC/person-month or FP/person-month)
- Combine function estimates to produce an overall estimate for the entire project

5. COCOMO Model (Empirical Process Model)

- Stands for **Constructive Cost Model**
- As with all estimation models, it requires sizing information and accepts it in three forms: object points, function points, and lines of source code
- **Application composition model** - Used during the early stages of software engineering when the following are important

- Prototyping of user interfaces
- Consideration of software and system interaction
- Assessment of performance
- Evaluation of technology maturity

- **Early design stage model** – Used once requirements have been stabilized and basic software architecture has been established
- **Post-architecture stage model** – Used during the construction of the software

Organic, Semidetached and Embedded software projects

- **Organic:** A development project can be considered of organic type, if the project deals with developing a well understood application program, the size of the development team is reasonably small, and the team members are experienced in developing similar types of projects.
- **Semidetached:** A development project can be considered of semidetached type, if the development consists of a mixture of experienced and inexperienced

staff. Team members may have limited experience on related systems but may be unfamiliar with some aspects of the system being developed.

- **Embedded:** A development project is considered to be of embedded type, if the software being developed is strongly coupled to complex hardware, or if the stringent regulations on the operational procedures exist.

The basic COCOMO model gives an approximate estimate of the project parameters. The basic COCOMO estimation model is given by following expressions:

Effort = a1 x (KLOC)a2 PM (person Month)

Time of Development = b1 x (Effort) b2 Months

Where, a1,a2,b1,b2 are constants for each category of software products

Estimation of Effort

Organic: Effort = 2.4 (KLOC) 1.05 PM Semi-detached: Effort = 3.0 (KLOC) 1.12 PM Embedded: Effort = 3.6 (KLOC) 1.20 PM **Estimation Time of Development**

Organic: Time of Development = 2.5 (Effort) 0.38 Months

Semi-detached: Time of Development = 2.5 (Effort) 0.35 Months Embedded: Time of Development = 2.5 (Effort) 0.32 Months

Example:

Assume that the size of an organic s/w product has been estimated to be 32,000 lines of source code. Assume that the average salary of software be Rs. 15,000/- month. Determine the effort required to develop the software product and the nominal development time.

Effort= 2.4 x (32) 1.05 = 91 PM

Time of development = 2.5 x (91) 0.38 = 14 months

Cost= 14 x 15,000 = Rs. 2,10,000/-

6. Software Project Planning

- The objective of software project planning is to provide a framework that enables the manager to make reasonable estimates of resources, cost, and schedule.
- In addition, estimates should attempt to define best-case and worst-case scenarios so that project outcomes can be bounded. Although there is an inherent degree of uncertainty, the software team embarks on a plan that has been established as a consequence of these tasks.
- Therefore, the plan must be adapted and updated as the project proceeds.

Task Set for Project Planning

1. Establish project scope.
2. Determine feasibility.
3. Analyze risks.
4. Define required resources.

   a. Determine required human resources.
   b. Define reusable software resources.
   c. Identify environmental resources.

5. Estimate cost and effort.

   a. Decompose the problem.

b. Develop two or more estimates using size, function points, process tasks, or use cases.
c. Reconcile the estimates.

6. Develop a project schedule.

   a. Establish a meaningful task set.
   b. Define a task network.
   c. Use scheduling tools to develop a time-line chart.
   d. Define schedule tracking mechanisms.

7. Project Scheduling

- Software project scheduling is an action that distributes estimated effort across the planned project duration by allocating the effort to specific software engineering tasks.
- It is important to note, however, that the schedule evolves over time.
- During early stages of project planning, a macroscopic schedule is developed.
- This type of schedule identifies all major process framework activities and the product functions to which they are applied.

Scheduling Principles

- <u>Compartmentalization</u>

The product and process must be decomposed into a manageable number of activities and tasks

- <u>Interdependency</u>

  Tasks that can be completed in parallel must be separated from those that must completed serially

- <u>Time allocation</u>

  Every task has start and completion dates that take the task interdependencies into account

- <u>Effort validation</u>

  Project manager must ensure that on any given day there are enough staff members assigned to completed the tasks within the time estimated in the project plan

- <u>Defined Responsibilities</u>

  Every scheduled task needs to be assigned to a specific team member

- <u>Defined outcomes</u>

  Every task in the schedule needs to have a defined outcome (usually a work product or deliverable)

- <u>Defined milestones</u>

  A milestone is accomplished when one or more work products from an engineering task have passed quality review

Scheduling

- Scheduling of a software project does not differ greatly from scheduling of any multitask engineering effort.
- Therefore, generalized project scheduling tools and techniques can be applied with little modification for software projects.
- Program evaluation and review technique (PERT) and the critical path method (CPM) are two project scheduling methods that can be applied to software development.
- Both techniques are driven by information already developed in earlier project planning activities: estimates of effort, a decomposition of the product function, the selection of the appropriate process model and task set, and decomposition of the tasks that are selected.
- Both PERT and CPM provide quantitative tools that allow you to

  1. Determine the critical path—the chain of tasks that determines the duration of the project
  2. Establish "most likely" time estimates for individual tasks by applying statistical models
  3. Calculate "boundary times" that define a time "window" for a particular task.

8. Project Tracking

- The project schedule provides a road map for a software project manager.
- It defines the tasks and milestones.

- Several ways to track a project schedule:

- conducting periodic project status meeting
- evaluating the review results in the software process
- determine if formal project milestones have been accomplished
- compare actual start date to planned start date for each task
- informal meeting with practitioners

- Project manager takes the control of the schedule in the aspects of:

- project staffing
- project problems
- project resources
- reviews
- project budget

9. Risk Management

- A risk is a potential problem – it might happen and it might not
- Conceptual definition of risk

- Risk concerns future happenings
- Risk involves change in mind, opinion, actions, places, etc.
- Risk involves choice and the uncertainty that choice entails

- Two characteristics of risk

Uncertainty – the risk may or may not happen, that is, there are no 100% risks (those, instead, are called constraints)

Loss – the risk becomes a reality and unwanted consequences or losses occur

Categories of risk

- Project risks

- They threaten the project plan
- If they become real, it is likely that the project schedule will slip and that costs will increase

- Technical risks

- They threaten the quality and timeliness of the software to be produced
- If they become real, implementation may become difficult or impossible

- Business risks

- They threaten the feasibility of the software to be built
- If they become real, they threaten the project or the product

- Known risks

– Those risks that can be uncovered after careful evaluation of the project plan, the business and technical environment in which the project is being developed, and other reliable information sources (e.g., unrealistic delivery date)

- Predictable risks

  – Those risks that are deduced from past project experience (e.g., past turnover)

- Unpredictable risks

  – Those risks that can and do occur, but are extremely difficult to identify in advance

Sub-Categories of risk

- **Market risk** – building an excellent product or system that no one really wants
- **Strategic risk** – building a product that no longer fits into the overall business strategy for the company
- **Sales risk** – building a product that the sales force doesn't understand how to sell
- **Management risk** – losing the support of senior management due to a change in focus or a change in people
- **Budget risk** – losing budgetary or personnel commitment

Risk Identification

- One method for identifying risks is to create a risk item checklist.
- The checklist can be used for risk identification and focuses on some subset of known and predictable risks in the following generic subcategories:
- Product size—risks associated with the overall size of the software to be built or modified.
- Business impact—risks associated with constraints imposed by management or the marketplace.
- Stakeholder characteristics—risks associated with the sophistication of the stakeholders and the developer's ability to communicate with stakeholders in a timely manner.
- Process definition—risks associated with the degree to which the software process has been defined and is followed by the development organization.
- Development environment—risks associated with the availability and quality of the tools to be used to build the product.
- Technology to be built—risks associated with the complexity of the system to be built and the "newness" of the technology that is packaged by the system.
- Staff size and experience—risks associated with the overall technical and project experience of the software engineers who will do the work.

10. Risk Estimation / Risk Projection

Risk Projection Steps

- Establish a scale that reflects the perceived likelihood of a risk (e.g., 1-low, 10-high)
- Explain the consequences of the risk
- Estimate the impact of the risk on the project and product
- Note the overall accuracy of the risk projection so that there will be no misunderstandings

Risk Mitigation, Monitoring, and Management

- Risk mitigation (proactive planning for risk avoidance)
- Risk monitoring (assessing whether predicted risks occur or not, ensuring risk aversion steps are being properly applied, collect information for future risk analysis, attempt to determine which risks caused which problems)
- Risk management and contingency planning (actions to be taken in the event that mitigation steps have failed and the risk has become a live problem)
- The goal of the risk mitigation, monitoring and management plan is to identify as many potential risks as possible.
- When all risks have been identified, they will then be evaluated to determine their probability of occurrence,
- Plans will then be made to avoid each risk, to track each risk to determine if it is more or less likely to occur, and to plan for those risks should they occur.
- It is the organization's responsibility to perform risk mitigation, monitoring, and management in order to

produce a quality product.

- The quicker the risks can be identified and avoided, the smaller the chances of having to face that particular risk's consequence.
- The fewer consequences suffered as a result of good RMMM plan, the better the product, and the smoother the development process.

Risk Mitigation

- To mitigate this risk, you would develop a strategy for reducing turnover. Among the possible steps to be taken are:
- Meet with current staff to determine causes for turnover (e.g., poor working conditions, low pay, and competitive job market).
- Mitigate those causes that are under your control before the project starts.
- Once the project commences, assume turnover will occur and develop techniques to ensure continuity when people leave.
- Organize project teams so that information about each development activity is widely dispersed.
- Define work product standards and establish mechanisms to be sure that all models and documents are developed in a timely manner.
- Conduct peer reviews of all work (so that more than one person is "up to speed").
- Assign a backup staff member for every critical technologist.

Risk Monitoring

- The project manager monitors factors that may provide an indication of whether the risk is becoming more or less likely.
- In the case of high staff turnover, the general attitude of team members based on project pressures, the degree to which the team has jelled, inter-personal relationships among team members, potential problems with compensation and benefits, and the availability of jobs within the company and outside it are all monitored.
- In addition to monitoring these factors, a project manager should monitor the effectiveness of risk mitigation steps.
- The project manager should monitor work products carefully to ensure that each can stand on its own and that each imparts information that would be necessary if a newcomer were forced to join the software team somewhere in the middle of the project.

Risk Management

- Risk management and contingency planning assumes that mitigation efforts have failed and that the risk has become a reality.
- If the mitigation strategy has been followed, backup is available, information is documented, and knowledge has been dispersed across the team.

- In addition, you can temporarily refocus resources (and readjust the project schedule) to those functions that are fully staffed, enabling newcomers who must be added to the team to "get up to speed." Those individuals who are leaving are asked to stop all work and spend their last weeks in "knowledge transfer mode."

11. The W5HH Principle for Project Management

- Boehm suggests an approach that addresses project objectives, milestones and schedules, responsibilities, management and technical approaches, and required resources.
- He calls it the W^5HH Principle, after a series of questions that lead to a definition of key project characteristics and the resultant project plan
- W5HH Principle is applicable regardless of the size or complexity of a software project.
- The questions noted provide you and your team with an excellent planning outline.
- *Why is the system being developed?* All stakeholders should assess the validity of business reasons for the software work. Does the business purpose justify the expenditure of people, time, and money?
- *What will be done?* The task set required for the project is defined.
- *When will it be done?* The team establishes a project schedule by identifying when project tasks are to be conducted and when milestones are to be reached.
- *Who is responsible for a function?* The role and responsibility of each member of the software team is defined.

- ***Where*** *are they located organizationally?* Not all roles and responsibilities reside within software practitioners. The customer, users, and other stakeholders also have responsibilities.
- ***How*** *will the job be done technically and managerially?* Once product scope is established, a management and technical strategy for the project must be defined.

How *much of each resource is needed?* The answer to this question is derived by developing estimates based on answers to earlier questions.

CHAPTER FOUR

Requirement Analysis and Specification

1. Requirement Engineering Process

- Requirement Engineering means that requirements for a product are defined, managed and tested systematically.
- Requirements engineering builds a bridge to design and construction.
- Requirements engineering provides the appropriate mechanism for understanding what the customer wants, analyzing need, assessing feasibility, negotiating a reasonable solution, specifying the solution unambiguously, validating the specification, and managing the requirements as they are transformed into an operational system.

Requirement Engineering Tasks

- Inception

–Establish a basic understanding of the problem and the nature of the solution.

– In project inception, you establish a basic understanding of the problem, the people who want a solution, the nature of the solution that is desired, and the effectiveness of preliminary communication and collaboration between the other stakeholders and the software team.

• Elicitation

–Draw out the requirements from stakeholders.

–Number of problems that are encountered as elicitation occurs are problems of scope, problems of understanding, problems of volatility

• **Elaboration** (Highly structured)

–Create an analysis model that represents information, functional, and behavioral aspects of the requirements.

–Elaboration is driven by the creation and refinement of user scenarios that describe how the end user (and other actors) will interact with the system.

– Each user scenario is parsed to extract analysis classes—business domain entities that are visible to the end user.

–The attributes of each analysis class are defined, and the services that are required by each class are identified.

–The relationships and collaboration between classes are identified, and a variety of supplementary diagrams are produced.

- Negotiation

  − Agree on a deliverable system that is realistic for developers and customers.

  −The best negotiations strive for a "win-win" result.

  − That is, stakeholders win by getting the system or product that satisfies the majority of their needs and you (as a member of the software team) win by working to realistic and achievable budgets and deadlines.

  −activities in negotiation are :

  − Identification of the system or subsystem's key stakeholders.

  −Determination of the stakeholders' "win conditions."

  − Negotiation of the stakeholders' win conditions to reconcile them into a set of win-win conditions for all concerned (including the software team).

- Specification

  −Describe the requirements formally or informally.

  − A specification can be a written document, a set of graphical models, a formal mathematical model, and a collection of usage scenarios, a prototype, or any combination of these.

- Validation

  − Review the requirement specification for errors, ambiguities, omissions, and conflicts.

  −Requirements validation examines the specification to ensure that all software requirements have been stated unambiguously; that inconsistencies, omissions, and errors have been detected and corrected; and that the work products conform to the standards established for the process, the project, and the product.

–The primary requirements validation mechanism is the technical review.

–The review team that validates requirements includes software engineers, customers, users, and other stakeholders who examine the specification looking for errors in content or interpretation, areas where clarification may be required, missing information, inconsistencies (a major problem when large products or systems are engineered), conflicting requirements, or unrealistic (unachievable) requirements.

- Requirements management

–Manage changing requirements.

– Requirements management is a set of activities that help the project team identify, control, and track requirements and changes to requirements at any time as the project process.

–Many of these activities are identical to the software configuration management.

1. Requirement Elicitation

- Requirements elicitation (also called requirements gathering) combines elements of problem solving, elaboration, negotiation, and specification.
- In order to encourage a collaborative, team-oriented approach to requirements gathering, stakeholders work together to identify the problem, propose elements of

the solution, negotiate different approaches and specify a preliminary set of solution requirements.

Collaborative Requirements Gathering

- The goal is to identify the problem, propose elements of the solution, negotiate different approaches, and specify a preliminary set of solution requirements in an atmosphere that is conducive to the accomplishment of the goal.
- Meetings are conducted and attended by both software engineers and other stakeholders.
- Rules for preparation and participation are established.
- An agenda is suggested that is formal enough to cover all important points but informal enough to encourage the free flow of ideas.
- A "facilitator" (can be a customer, a developer, or an outsider) controls the meeting.
- A "definition mechanism" (can be work sheets, flip charts, or wall stickers or an electronic bulletin board, chat room, or virtual forum) is used.

Quality Function Deployment

- Quality function deployment (QFD) is a quality management technique that translates the needs of the customer into technical requirements for software. QFD "concentrates on maximizing customer satisfaction from the software engineering process".

- QFD identifies three types of requirements normal requirements, expected requirements, exciting requirements

Usage Scenarios

- As requirements are gathered, an overall vision of system functions and features begins to materialize.
- Users can create a set of scenarios that identify a thread of usage for the system to be constructed.
- The scenarios, often called use cases.

Elicitation Work Products

- The work products produced as a consequence of requirements elicitation will vary depending on the size of the system or product to be built. For most systems, the work products include
- A statement of need and feasibility.
- A bounded statement of scope for the system or product.
- A list of customers, users, and other stakeholders who participated in requirements elicitation.
- A description of the system's technical environment.
- A list of requirements (preferably organized by function) and the domain constraints that apply to each.
- A set of usage scenarios that provide insight into the use of the system or product under different operating conditions.

- Any prototypes developed to better define requirements.

3. System Requirement Specification

- It contains a complete information description, a detailed functional description, a representation of system behaviour, an indication of performance requirements and design constraints, appropriate validation criteria, and other information pertinent to requirements.
- Software requirement specification (SRS) is a document that completely describes what the proposed software should do without describing how software will do it.
- The basic goal of the requirement phase is to produce the SRS, Which describes the complete behaviour of the proposed software.
- SRS is also helping the clients to understand their own needs.

Characteristics of an SRS

Software requirements specification should be accurate, complete, efficient, and of high quality, so that it does not affect the entire project plan. An SRS is said to be of high quality when the developer and user easily understand the prepared document. Other characteristics of SRS are discussed below.

Correct

- SRS is correct when all user requirements are stated in the requirements document.

- The stated requirements should be according to the desired system.
- This implies that each requirement is examined to ensure that it (SRS) represents user requirements.
- Note that there is no specified tool or procedure to assure the correctness of SRS. Correctness ensures that all specified requirements are performed correctly.

Unambiguous

- SRS is unambiguous when every stated requirement has only one interpretation.
- This implies that each requirement is uniquely interpreted.
- In case there is a term used with multiple meanings, the requirements document should specify the meanings in the SRS so that it is clear and easy to understand.

Complete

- SRS is complete when the requirements clearly define what the software is required to do.
- This includes all the requirements related to performance, design and functionality.

Ranked for importance/stability

- All requirements are not equally important, hence each requirement is identified to make differences among other requirements.
- For this, it is essential to clearly identify each requirement. Stability implies the probability of changes in the requirement in future.

Modifiable

- The requirements of the user can change, hence requirements document should be created in such a manner that those changes can be modified easily, consistently maintaining the structure and style of the SRS.

Traceable

- SRS is traceable when the source of each requirement is clear and facilitates the reference of each requirement in future.
- For this, forward tracing and backward tracing are used.
- Forward tracing implies that each requirement should be traceable to design and code elements.
- Backward tracing implies defining each requirement explicitly referencing its source.

Verifiable

- SRS is verifiable when the specified requirements can be verified with a cost-effective process to check whether the final software meets those requirements.
- The requirements are verified with the help of reviews. Note that unambiguity is essential for verifiability.

Consistent

- SRS is consistent when the subsets of individual requirements defined do not conflict with each other.
- For example, there can be a case when different requirements can use different terms to refer to the

same object.

- There can be logical or temporal conflicts between the specified requirements and some requirements whose logical or temporal characteristics are not satisfied.
- For instance, a requirement states that an event 'a' is to occur before another event 'b'. But then another set of requirements states (directly or indirectly by transitivity) that event 'b' should occur before event 'a'.

4. Functional and Non-Functional Requirements

Functional requirements

- These describe the functionality of a system -- how a system should react to a particular set of inputs and what should be the corresponding output.
- Given a problem statement, the functional requirements could be identified by focusing on the following points:

–Identify the high level functional requirements simply from the conceptual understanding of the problem. For example, a Library Management System, apart from anything else, should be able to issue and return books.

– Identify the cases where an end user gets some meaningful work done by using the system. For example, in a digital library a user might use the "Search Book" functionality to obtain information about the books of his interest.

–If we consider the system as a black box, there would be some inputs to it, and some output in return. This black box defines the functionalities of the system. For example, to search for a book, user gives title of the book as input and get the book details and location as the output.

– Any high level requirement identified could have different sub-requirements. For example, "Issue Book" module could behave differently for different class of users, or for a particular user who has issued the book thrice consecutively.

Non-Functional requirements

- They are not directly related what functionalities are expected from the system.
- However, NFRs could typically define how the system should behave under certain situations.
- For example, a NFR could say that the system should work with 128MB RAM.

Product requirements

- Requirements which specify that the delivered product must behave in a particular way e.g. execution speed, reliability, etc.

Organisational requirements

- Requirements which are a consequence of organisational policies and procedures e.g. process standards used, implementation requirements, etc.

External requirements

- Requirements which arise from factors which are external to the system and its development process e.g. interoperability requirements, legislative requirements, etc.

Example:

Functional Requirements for Hotel Management System

1. Reservation/Booking

   1. The system shall record reservations.
   2. The system shall record the customer's first name.
   3. The system shall record the customer's last name.
   4. The system shall record the number of occupants.
   5. The system shall record the room number.
   6. The system shall display the default room rate.
   7. The system shall record the customer's phone number.
   8. The system shall display whether or not the room is guaranteed.
   9. The system shall generate a unique confirmation number for each reservation.
   10. The system shall record the expected check-in date and time.
   11. The system shall record the expected checkout date and time.
   12. The system shall check-in customers.

   13. The system shall allow reservations to be modified without having to reenter all the customer information.
   14. The system shall checkout customers.
   15. The system shall charge the customer for an extra night if they checkout after 11:00 a.m.
   16. The system shall mark guaranteed rooms as "must pay" after 6:00 PM on the check-in date.

17. The system shall record customer feedback.

2. Food

    1. The system shall track all meals purchased in the hotel (restaurant and room service).
    2. The system shall record payment and payment type for meals.
    3. The system shall bill the current room if payment is not made at time of service.
    4. The system shall accept reservations for the restaurant and room service.

3. Management

    1. The system shall display the hotel occupancy for a specified period of time (days; including past, present, and future dates).
    2. The system shall display projected occupancy for a period of time (days).
    3. The system shall display room revenue for a specified period of time (days).
    4. The system shall display food revenue for a specified period of time (days).
    5. The system shall display an exception report, showing where default room and food prices have been overridden.
    6. The system shall allow for the addition of information, regarding rooms, rates, menu items, prices, and user profiles.
    7. The system shall allow for the deletion of information, regarding rooms, rates, menu items, prices, and user profiles.

8. The system shall allow for the modification of information, regarding rooms, rates, menu items, prices, and user profiles.
9. The system shall allow managers to assign user passwords.

Non-Functional Requirements for Hotel Management System

1. The load time for user interface screens shall take no longer than two seconds.
2. The log in information shall be verified within five seconds.
3. Queries shall return results within five seconds.
4. The Hotel Management System shall be a stand-alone system running in a Windows environment.
5. The system shall be developed using Java platform.
6. There shall be consistency in variable names within the system.
7. The graphical user interface shall have a consistent look and feel.
8. Specify the factors required to establish the required reliability of the software system at time of delivery.
9. The system shall be available during normal hotel operating hours.
10. Customer Service Representatives and Managers will be able to log in to the Hotel Management System. Customer Service Representatives will have access to the Reservation/Booking and Food subsystems. Managers will have access to the Management subsystem as well as the Reservation/Booking and Food

subsystems.

11. Access to the various subsystems will be protected by a user log in screen that requires a user name and password.

5. Feasibility Study

Feasibility study establishes the basic business requirements and constraints associated with the application to be built and then assesses whether the application is a viable candidate for the process.

Types of Feasibility Study

Technical feasibility

- In technical feasibility analysis, alternatives for hardware, software and general design approach are determined to be available, appropriate, and functional.

The technical issues raised during the feasibility study are:

a. Does the necessary technology exist?
b. Does the proposed equipment have the technical capacity to hold the data required to use the new system?
c. Will the proposed system and components provide adequate responses to enquires, regardless of the number of location of users?
d. Can the system be expanded, if developed?
e. Are there technical guarantees of accuracy, reliability, ease of access and data security?

Operational feasibility

- Operational feasibility study tests the operational scope of the software to be developed. The proposed software must have high operational feasibility. The usability will be high.
- Operational feasibility is dependent on human resources available for the project and involves projecting whether the system will be used if it is developed and implemented.
- Operational feasibility is a measure of how well a proposed system solves the problems, and takes advantage of the opportunities identified during scope definition and how it satisfies the requirements identified in the requirements analysis phase of system development.

The essential questions that help in testing the operational feasibility of a system include the following:

a. Does current mode of operation provide adequate throughput and response time?
b. Does current mode provide end users and managers with timely, pertinent, accurate and useful formatted information?
c. Does current mode of operation provide cost-effective information services to the business?
d. Could there be a reduction in cost and or an increase in benefits?
e. Does current mode of operation offer effective controls to protect against fraud and to guarantee accuracy and security of data and information?

f. Does current mode of operation make maximum use of available resources, including people, time, and flow of forms?

g. Does current mode of operation provide reliable services

h. Are the services flexible and expandable?

a. Are the current work practices and procedures adequate to support the new system?

j. If the system is developed, will it be used?

k. Manpower problems, Labour objections, Manager resistance, Organizational conflicts and policies,

Government regulations

ax. Does management support the project?

all. Are the users not happy with current business practices?

n. Will it reduce the time (operation) considerably?

o. Have the users been involved in the planning and development of the project?

p. Will the proposed system really benefit the organization?

Economic feasibility

- The economic feasibility study evaluate the cost of the software development against the ultimate income or benefits gets from the developed system.
- There must be scopes for profit after the successful Completion of the project. Possible questions raised in economic analysis are:

a. Is the system cost effective?
b. Do benefits outweigh costs?
c. The cost of doing full system study
d. The cost of business employee time
e. Estimated cost of hardware
f. Estimated cost of software/software development
g. Is the project possible, given the resource constraints?
h. What are the savings that will result from the system?
a. Cost of employees' time for study.
j. Cost of packaged software/software development.

6. Use case Diagram Symbols and Examples

(I) ATM Machine (II) Library Management System
Use Case Notations
Name
Notation
Description
System boundary
System
The scope of a system can be represented by a system boundary. The use cases of the system are placed inside the system boundary, while the actors who interact with the system are put outside the system. The use cases in the system make up the total
requirements of the system.
Use case
UseCase1
A use case represents a user goal that can be achieved by accessing the system or software application.
Actor

Actor

Actors are the entities that interact with a system. Although in most cases, actors are used to represent the users of system, actors can actually be anything that needs to exchange information with the system. So an actor may be people, computer hardware, other systems, etc. Note that actor represent a role that a user can play,

but not a specific user.

Association

Actor and use case can be associated to indicate that the actor participates in that use case. Therefore, an association corresponds to a sequence of actions between the actor and use

case in achieving the use case.

Generalizatio n

A generalization relationship is used to represent inheritance relationship between model elements of same type.

Include

<<include>>

An include relationship specifies how the behavior for the inclusion use case is inserted into the behavior defined for the base use case.

Extends

<<Extends>>

An extend relationship specifies how the behavior of the extension

use case can be inserted into the behavior defined for the base use case.

Constraint

{condition}

Show condition exists between actors an activity.

Interface

Interface

Interface is used to connect package and use-case. Head is linked

with package and tail linked with use-case.

Anchor

Anchor is used to connect a note the use case in use case diagram

7. ER Diagram Symbols and Example

E-R Diagram Notations

Entity · Entities are objects or concepts that represent important data. They are typically nouns, e.g. customer, supervisor, location, or promotion.

- Strong entities exist independently from other entity types. They always possess one or more attributes that uniquely distinguish each occurrence of the entity.
- Weak entities depend on some other entity type. They don't possess unique attributes (also known as a primary key) and have no meaning in the diagram without depending on another entity.

Relationship · Relationships are meaningful associations between or among entities. They are usually verbs, e.g. assign,

associate, or track.

- Weak relationships, or identifying relationships, are connections that exist between a weak entity type and its owner.

Attributes · Attributes are

characteristics of either an entity, a many-to-many relationship, or a one-to- one relationship.

- Multivalued attributes are those that are capable of taking on more than one value.
- Derived attributes are attributes whose value can be calculated from related attribute values.

Association · Relationships illustrate an association

between two tables. In the physical data model, relationships are represented by
stylized lines.

- **<u>Cardinality and ordinality</u>**, respectively, refer to the maximum number of times an instance in one entity can be associated with instances in the related entity, and the minimum number of times an instance in one entity can be associated with an instance in the related entity. Cardinality and ordinality are represented by the styling of a line and its endpoint, as denoted by the chosen notation style

<u>ER Diagram for University Examination</u>

8. Context diagram and data flow diagram (DFD) for Airlines Reservation System.

Context diagram / Level 0 DFD

Level 1 DFD

Level 2 DFD

Software Design

1. Design Concepts and Principles

- Software design sits at the technical core of software engineering and is applied regardless of the software process model that is used.
- The design task produces a data design, an architectural design, an interface design, and a component design.

Data Design

- The data design transforms the information domain model created during analysis into the data structures that will be required to implement the software.
- The data objects and relationships defined in the entity relationship diagram.
- Part of data design may occur in combination with the design of software architecture.

Architectural Design

- The architectural design defines the relationship between major structural elements of the software.

- The architectural design representation—the framework of a computer-based system—can be derived from the system specification, the analysis model, and the interaction of subsystems defined within the analysis model.

Interface Design

- The interface design describes how the software communicates within itself, with systems that interoperate with it, and with humans who use it.
- An interface implies a flow of information (e.g., data and/or control) and a specific type of behavior. Therefore, data and control flow diagrams provide much of the information required for interface design.

Component-level Design

- The component-level design transforms structural elements of the software architecture into a procedural description of software components.

Design principles

1. The design process should not suffer from "tunnel vision."
2. The design should be traceable to the analysis model.
3. The design should not reinvent the wheel.
4. The design should "minimize the intellectual distance" between the software and the problem as it exists in the real world.
5. The design should exhibit uniformity and integration.

6. The design should be structured to accommodate change.
7. The design should be structured to degrade gently, even when abnormal data, events, or operating conditions are encountered.
8. Design is not coding, coding is not design.
9. The design should be assessed for quality as it is being created, not after the fact.
10. The design should be reviewed to minimize conceptual (semantic) errors.

1. Software architecture and software design

- Architectural design represents the structure of data and program components that are required to build a computer-based system.
- It considers the architectural style that the system will take, the structure and properties of the components
- that constitute the system, and the interrelationships that occur among all architectural components of a system.
- Representations of software architecture are an enabler for communication between all parties (stakeholders) interested in the development of a computer-based system.
- The architecture highlights early design decisions that will have a reflective impact on all software engineering work that follows and, as important, on the ultimate success of the system as an operational entity.

- Architecture "constitutes a relatively small, intellectually graspable model of how the system is structured and how its components work together"

Architectural Styles

The software that is built for computer-based systems also exhibits one of many architectural styles. Each style describes a system category that encompasses

1. A set of components (e.g., a database, computational modules) that perform a function required by a system.
2. A set of connectors that enable "communication, coordinations and cooperation" among components.
3. Constraints that define how components can be integrated to form the system.
4. Semantic models that enable a designer to understand the overall properties of a system by analyzing the known properties of its constituent parts.

Data-centered architecture style

- A data store (e.g., a file or database) resides at the center of this architecture and is accessed frequently by other components that update, add, delete, or otherwise modify data within the store.
- Client software accesses a central repository.
- In some cases the data repository is passive.
- That is, client software accesses the data independent of any changes to the data or the actions of other client software.

Data-flow architectures

Figure: Data-centered architecture

- This architecture is applied when input data are to be transformed through a series of computational or manipulative components into output data.
- A pipe and filter pattern has a set of components, called filters, connected by pipes that transmit data from one component to the next.
- Each filter works independently of those components upstream and downstream, is designed to expect data input of a certain form, and produces data output (to the next filter) of a specified form.

- However, the filter does not require knowledge of the working of its neighboring filters.

Call and return architecture
Figure: Data-flow architectures

- This architectural style enables a software designer (system architect) to achieve a program structure that is relatively easy to modify and scale.

A number of sub styles exist within this category:

- *Main program/subprogram architectures*. This classic program structure decomposes function into a control hierarchy where a "main" program invokes a number of program components, which in turn may invoke still other components.
- *Remote procedure call architectures*. The components of a main program/ subprogram architecture are distributed across multiple computers on a network.

Object-oriented architecture

- The components of a system encapsulate data and the operations that must be applied to manipulate the data.
- Communication and coordination between components is accomplished via message passing.

Layered architecture

- A number of different layers are defined, each accomplishing operations that progressively become closer to the machine instruction set.
- At the outer layer, components service user interface operations.
- At the inner layer, components perform operating system interfacing.
- Intermediate layers provide utility services and application software functions.

3. Data Design

This section describes data design at both the architectural and component levels. At the architecture level, data design is the process of creating a model of the information represented at a high level of abstraction (using the customer's view of data).

Data Design at the Architectural Level

*   The challenge is extract useful information from the data environment, particularly when the information desired is cross-functional.

- To solve this challenge, the business IT community has developed data mining techniques, also called knowledge discovery in databases (KDD), that navigate through existing databases in an attempt to extract appropriate business-level information.
- However, the existence of multiple databases, their different structures, and the degree of detail contained with the databases, and many other factors make data mining difficult within an existing database environment.
- An alternative solution, called a data warehouse, adds on additional layer to the data architecture.
- A data warehouse is a separate data environment that is not directly integrated with day-to-day applications that encompasses all data used by a business.

Data Design at the Component Level

At the component level, data design focuses on specific data structures required to realize the data objects to be manipulated by a component.

– Refine data objects and develop a set of data abstractions

–Implement data object attributes as one or more data structures

– Review data structures to ensure that appropriate relationships have been established Set of principles for data specification:

1. The systematic analysis principles applied to function and behavior should also be applied to data.

2. All data structures and the operations to be performed on each should be identified.

3. A data dictionary should be established and used to define both data and program design.

4. Low level data design decisions should be deferred until late in the design process.

5. The representation of data structure should be known only to those modules that must make direct use of the data contained within the structure.

6. A library of useful data structures and the operations that may be applied to them should be developed.

7. A software design and programming language should support the specification and realization of abstract data types.

4. Component-Level Design or Procedural Design

- Component-level design, also called procedural design, occurs after data, architectural, and interface designs have been established.

- Component-level design defines the data structures, algorithms, interface characteristics, and communication mechanisms allocated to each software component.

- The intent is to translate the design model into operational software.

- But the level of abstraction of the existing design model is relatively high, and the abstraction level of the operational program is low.

- *Component* a modular, deployable, and replaceable part of a system that encapsulates implementation and exposes a set of interfaces."

Function Oriented Approach

The following are the salient features of a typical function-oriented design approach:

1. A system is viewed as something that performs a set of functions. Starting at this highlevel view of the system, each function is successively refined into more detailed functions.

   For example, consider a function create-new-library member which essentially creates the record for a new member, assigns a unique membership number to him, and prints a bill towards his membership charge. This function may consist of the following sub-functions:

   –assign-membership-number

   –create-member-record

   –print-bill

   Each of these sub-functions may be split into more detailed sub-functions and so on.

2. The system state is centralized and shared among different functions, e.g. data such as member- records is available for reference and updating to several functions such as:

   –create-new-member

   –delete-member

   –update-member-record

Object Oriented Approach

- In the object-oriented design approach, the system is viewed as collection of objects (i.e. entities). The state is decentralized among the objects and each object manages its own state information.
- For example, in a Library Automation Software, each library member may be a separate object with its own data and functions to operate on these data. In fact, the functions defined for one object cannot refer or change data of other objects.
- Objects have their own internal data which define their state. Similar objects constitute a class.
- In other words, each object is a member of some class. Classes may inherit features from super class. Conceptually, objects communicate by message passing.

Function-Oriented Vs. Object-Oriented Design

- Unlike function-oriented design methods, in OOD, the basic abstraction are not real world functions such as sort, display, track, etc., but real-world entities such as employee, picture, machine, radar system, etc.
- For example in OOD, an employee pay-roll software is not developed by designing functions such as update-employee record, get-employee-address, etc. but by designing objects such as employees, departments, etc.
- In object-oriented design, software is not developed by designing functions such as update-employee- record,

get-employee-address, etc., but by designing objects such as employee, department, etc.

- In OOD, state information is not represented in a centralized shared memory but is distributed among the objects of the system.

- For example, while developing an employee pay-roll system, the employee data such as the names of the employees, their code numbers, basic salaries, etc. are usually implemented as global data in a traditional programming system; whereas in an object-oriented system these data are distributed among different employee objects of the system.

- Objects communicate by passing messages. Therefore, one object may discover the state information of another object by interrogating it. Of course, somewhere or the other the real-world functions must be implemented.

- Function-oriented techniques such as SA/SD group functions together if, as a group, they constitute a higher-level function. On the other hand, object-oriented techniques group functions together on the basis of the data they operate on.

5. Cohesion and Coupling

- *Cohesion* is an indication of the relative functional strength of a module.

- A cohesive module performs a single task, requiring little interaction with other components in other parts of a program. Stated simply, a cohesive module should (ideally) do just one thing.

- Cohesion is a measure of functional strength of a module.

- A module having high cohesion and low coupling is said to be functionally independent of other modules. By the term functional independence, we mean that a cohesive module performs a single task or function.
- *Coupling* is an indication of the relative interdependence among modules.
- Coupling depends on the interface complexity between modules, the point at which entry or reference is made to a module, and what data pass across the interface.
- A module having high cohesion and low coupling is said to be functionally independent of other modules. If two modules interchange large amounts of data, then they are highly interdependent.
- The degree of coupling between two modules depends on their interface complexity.

Classification Cohesion

Coincidental cohesion

- A module is said to have coincidental cohesion, if it performs a set of tasks that relate to each other very loosely, if at all.
- In this case, the module contains a random collection of functions. It is likely that the functions have been put in the module out of pure coincidence without any thought or design.

- For example, in a transaction processing system (TPS), the get-input, print-error, and summarize- members
- functions are grouped into one module.

Logical cohesion

- A module is said to be logically cohesive, if all elements of the module perform similar operations, e.g. error handling, data input, data output, etc.
- An example of logical cohesion is the case where a set of print functions generating different output reports are arranged into a single module.

Temporal cohesion

- When a module contains functions that are related by the fact that all the functions must be executed in the same time span, the module is said to exhibit temporal cohesion.
- The set of functions responsible for initialization, start-up, shutdown of some process, etc. exhibit temporal cohesion.

Procedural cohesion

- A module is said to possess procedural cohesion, if the set of functions of the module are all part of a procedure (algorithm) in which certain sequence of steps have to be carried out for achieving an objective, e.g. the algorithm for decoding a message.

Communicational cohesion

- A module is said to have communicational cohesion, if all functions of the module refer to or update the same data structure, e.g. the set of functions defined on an array or a stack.

Sequential cohesion

- A module is said to possess sequential cohesion, if the elements of a module form the parts of sequence, where the output from one element of the sequence is input to the next.
- For example, in a TPS, the get-input, validate-input, sort-input functions are grouped into one module.

Functional cohesion

- Functional cohesion is said to exist, if different elements of a module cooperate to achieve a single function. For example, a module containing all the functions required to manage employees' pay-roll exhibits functional cohesion.
- Suppose a module exhibits functional cohesion and we are asked to describe what the module does, then we would be able to describe it using a single sentence.

Classification of Coupling

Data coupling

- Two modules are data coupled, if they communicate through a parameter. An example is an elementary data item passed as a parameter between two modules, e.g. an integer, a float, a character, etc.
- This data item should be problem related and not used for the control purpose.

Stamp coupling

- Two modules are stamp coupled, if they communicate using a composite data item such as a record in PASCAL or a structure in C.

Control coupling

- Control coupling exists between two modules, if data from one module is used to direct the order of instructions execution in another.
- An example of control coupling is a flag set in one module and tested in another module.

Common coupling

- Two modules are common coupled, if they share data through some global data items.

Content coupling

- Content coupling exists between two modules, if they share code, e.g. a branch from one module into another module.

6. User Interface Design

- *User interface design* creates an effective communication medium between a human and a computer.
- Following a set of interface design principles, design identifies interface objects and actions and then creates a screen layout that forms the basis for a user interface prototype.

Design Rules for User Interface

1. Place the User in Control

During a requirements-gathering session for a major new information system, a key user was asked about Following are the *design principles* that allow the user to maintain control:

−Define interaction modes in a way that does not force a user into unnecessary or undesired actions.

An interaction mode is the current state of the interface. For example, if spell check is selected in a word-processor menu, the software moves to a spell-checking mode. There is no reason to force the user to remain in spell-checking mode if the user desires to make a small text edit along the way.

−Provide for flexible interaction.

Because different users have different interaction preferences, choices should be provided. For example, software might allow a user to interact via keyboard commands, mouse movement, a digitizer pen, a multi touch screen, or voice recognition commands.

−Allow user interaction to be interruptible and undoable.

Even when involved in a sequence of actions, the user should be able to interrupt the sequence to do something else.

–Streamline interaction as skill levels advance and allow the interaction to be customized.

Users often find that they perform the same sequence of interactions repeatedly.

–Hide technical internals from the casual user.

The user interface should move the user into the virtual world of the application. The user should not be aware of the operating system, file management functions, or other arcane computing technology.

–Design for direct interaction with objects that appear on the screen.

The user feels a sense of control when able to manipulate the objects that are necessary to perform a task in a manner similar to what would occur if the object were a physical thing.

2. Reduce the User's Memory Load

The more a user has to remember, the more error-prone the interaction with the system will be. Following are the design principles that enable an interface to reduce the user's memory load:

–Reduce demand on short-term memory.

When users are involved in complex tasks, the demand on short-term memory can be significant. The interface should be designed to reduce the requirement to remember past actions, inputs, and results.

–**Establish meaningful defaults**.

The initial set of defaults should make sense for the average user, but a user should be able to specify individual preferences. However, a "reset" option should be available, enabling the redefinition of original default values.

–Define shortcuts that are intuitive.

When mnemonics are used to accomplish a system function, the mnemonic should be tied to the action in a way that is easy to remember.

–The visual layout of the interface should be based on a real-world metaphor.

This enables the user to rely on well-understood visual cues, rather than memorizing an arcane interaction sequence.

–Disclose information in a progressive fashion.

The interface should be organized hierarchically. That is, information about a task, an object, or some behavior should be presented first at a high level of abstraction.

3. Make the Interface Consistent

The interface should present and acquire information in a consistent fashion. Following are the design principles that help make the interface consistent:

–Allow the user to put the current task into a meaningful context.

Many interfaces implement complex layers of interactions with dozens of screen images. It is important to provide indicators that enable the user to know the context of the work at hand.

–Maintain consistency across a family of applications.

A set of applications should all implement the same design rules so that consistency is maintained for all interaction.

– If past interactive models have created user expectations, do not make changes unless there is a compelling reason to do so.

Once a particular interactive sequence has become a de facto standard, the user expects this in every application he encounters.

User Interface Design Models

Four different models come into play when a user interface is analyzed and designed.

1. User profile model – Established by a human engineer or software engineer

–Establishes the profile of the end-users of the system Based on age, gender, physical abilities, education, cultural or ethnic background, motivation, goals, and personality.

– The underlying sense of the application; an understanding of the functions that are performed, the meaning of input and output, and the objectives of the system Categorizes users as

Novices: No syntactic knowledge of the system, little semantic knowledge of the application, only general computer usage.

Knowledgeable, intermittent users: Reasonable semantic knowledge of the system, low recall of syntactic information to use the interface.

Knowledgeable, frequent users:

Good semantic and syntactic knowledge (i.e., power user), look for shortcuts and abbreviated modes of operation.

2. Design model – Created by a software engineer

    –Derived from the analysis model of the requirements Incorporates data, architectural, interface, and procedural representations of the software.
    – Constrained by information in the requirements specification that helps define the user of the system.

3. Implementation model – Created by the software implementers

    –Consists of the look and feel of the interface combined with all supporting information (books, videos, help files) that describe system syntax and semantics.
    – Strives to agree with the user's mental model; users then feel comfortable with the software and use it effectively.

4. User's mental model – Developed by the user when interacting with the application

    –Often called the user's system perception. Consists of the image of the system that users carry in their heads.
    – Accuracy of the description depends upon the user's profile and overall familiarity with the software in the application domain.
    The role of the interface designer is to merge these differences and derive a consistent representation of the interface.

(6) Web Application Design

Design for WebApp encompasses technical and nontechnical activities that include: establishing the look and feel of the WebApp, creating the aesthetic layout of the user interface, defining the overall architectural structure, developing the content and functionality that reside within the architecture, and planning the navigation that occurs within the WebApp.

WebApp Design Quality Requirement

Design is the engineering activity that leads to a high-quality product. This leads us to a recurring question that is encountered in all engineering disciplines.

Web App Interface Design

The objectives of a WebApp interface are to:

1. Establish a consistent window into the content and functionality provided by the interface.
2. Guide the user through a series of interactions with the WebApp.
3. Organize the navigation options and content available to the user.

Aesthetic Design

- Aesthetic design, also called graphic design, is an artistic endeavor that complements the technical aspects of WebApp design.
- Without it, a WebApp may be functional, but unappealing. With it, a WebApp draws its users into a world that embraces them on a primitive, as well as an intellectual level.

Content Design

- Content design focuses on two different design tasks, each addressed by individuals with different skill sets.
- First, a design representation for content objects and the mechanisms required to establish their relationship to one another is developed.
- In addition, the information within a specific content object is created.
- The latter task may be conducted by copywriters, graphic designers, and others who generate the content to be used within a WebApp.

Architecture Design

- Architecture design is tied to the goals established for a WebApp, the content to be presented, the users who will visit, and the navigation philosophy that has been established.

- In most cases, architecture design is conducted in parallel with interface design, aesthetic design, and content design.
- Because the WebApp architecture may have a strong influence on navigation, the decisions made during this design action will influence work conducted during navigation design.

Navigation Design

Once the WebApp architecture has been established and the components (pages, scripts, applets, and other processing functions) of the architecture have been identified, you must define navigation pathways that enable users to access WebApp content and functions.

Component-Level Design

Modern WebApps deliver increasingly sophisticated processing functions that

1. Perform localized processing to generate content and navigation capability in a dynamic fashion,
2. Provide computation or data processing capability that are appropriate for the WebApp's business domain.
3. Provide sophisticated database query and access.
4. Establish data interfaces with external corporate systems.

CHAPTER SIX

Software Coding & Testing-I

1. Coding Standard and coding Guidelines

Coding

- Good software development organizations normally require their programmers to adhere to some well-defined and standard style of coding called coding standards.

- Most software development organizations formulate their own coding standards that suit them most, and require their engineers to follow these standards rigorously.

- The purpose of requiring all engineers of an organization to adhere to a standard style of coding is the following:

–A coding standard gives a uniform appearance to the codes written by different engineers.

–It enhances code understanding.

–It encourages good programming practices.

- A coding standard lists several rules to be followed during coding, such as the way variables are to be named, the way the code is to be laid out, error return conventions, etc.

Coding standards and guidelines

The following are some representative coding standards.

Rules for limiting the use of global:

- These rules list what types of data can be declared global and what cannot.

Contents of the headers preceding codes for different modules:

- The information contained in the headers of different modules should be standard for an organization.
- The exact format in which the header information is organized in the header can also be specified.
- The following are some standard header data:

–Name of the module.

–Date on which the module was created.

–Modification history.

–Different functions supported, along with their input/output parameters.

–Global variables accessed/modified by the module.

Naming conventions for global variables, local variables, and constant identifiers:

- A possible naming convention can be that global variable names always start with a capital letter, local variable names are made of small letters, and constant names are always capital letters.

Error return conventions and exception handling mechanisms:

- The way error conditions are reported by different functions in a program are handled should be standard within an organization.

Do not use a coding style that is too clever or too difficult to understand:

- Code should be easy to understand. Many inexperienced engineers actually take pride in writing cryptic and incomprehensible code. Clever coding can ambiguous meaning of the code and delay understanding.

Avoid obscure side effects:

- The side effects of a function call include modification of parameters passed by reference, modification of global variables, and I/O operations.

- An unclear side effect is one that is not obvious from a casual examination of the code.

Do not use an identifier for multiple purposes:

- Programmers often use the same identifier to denote several temporary entities.
- For example, some programmers use a temporary loop variable for computing and a storing the final result.
- Each variable should be given a descriptive name indicating its purpose.

The code should be well-documented:

- As a rule of thumb, there must be at least one comment line on the average for every three-source line.

The length of any function should not exceed 10 source lines:

- A function that is very lengthy is usually very difficult to understand as it probably carries out many different functions.

Do not use goto statements:

- Use of goto statements makes a program unstructured and makes it very difficult to understand.

2. Code Review, Code Walk Through, Code Inspection

Code Review

- Code review for a model is carried out after the module is successfully compiled and the all the syntax errors have been eliminated.
- Code reviews are extremely cost-effective strategies for reduction in coding errors and to produce high quality code. Normally, two types of reviews are carried out on the code of a module.
- There are two types' code review techniques are code inspection and code walk through.

Code Walk Through

- Code walk through is an informal code analysis technique.
- In this technique, after a module has been coded, successfully compiled and all syntax errors eliminated.
- A few members of the development team are given the code few days before the walk through meeting to read and understand code.
- Each member selects some test cases and simulates execution of the code by hand.
- The main objectives of the walk through are to discover the algorithmic and logical errors in the code.
- Even though a code walk through is an informal analysis technique, several guidelines have evolved

over the years for making this naïve but useful analysis technique more effective.

Code Inspection

- In contrast to code walk through, the aim of code inspection is to discover some common types of errors caused due to oversight and improper programming.
- In other words, during code inspection the code is examined for the presence of certain kinds of errors, in contrast to the hand simulation of code execution done in code walk through.
- For instance, consider the classical error of writing a procedure that modifies a formal parameter while the calling routine calls that procedure with a constant actual parameter.
- It is more likely that such an error will be discovered by looking for these kinds of mistakes in the code, rather than by simply hand simulating execution of the procedure.
- In addition to the commonly made errors, adherence to coding standards is also checked during code inspection.
- Good software development companies collect statistics regarding different types of errors commonly committed by their engineers and identify the type of errors most frequently committed.

Software Documentation

- When various kinds of software products are developed then not only the executable files and the source code are developed but also various kinds of documents such as users' manual, software requirements specification (SRS) documents, design documents, test documents, installation manual, etc. are also developed as part of any software engineering process.
- All these documents are a vital part of good software development practice.
- Different types of software documents can broadly be classified into the following:

–Internal documentation
–External documentation

- Internal documentation is the code comprehension features provided as part of the source code itself.
- Internal documentation is provided through appropriate module headers and comments embedded in the source code.
- Internal documentation is also provided through the useful variable names, module and function headers, code indentation, code structuring, use of enumerated types and constant identifiers, use of user-defined data types, etc.
- This is of course in contrast to the common expectation that code commenting would be the most useful. The research finding is obviously true

when comments are written without thought.

- But even when code is carefully commented, meaningful variable names still are more helpful in understanding a piece of code. Good software development organizations usually ensure good internal documentation by appropriately formulating their coding standards and coding guidelines.
- External documentation is provided through various types of supporting documents such as users' manual, software requirements specification document, design document, test documents, etc.
- A systematic software development style ensures that all these documents are produced in an orderly fashion.

2. Testing Strategies

- *Software testing* is a critical element of software quality assurance and represents the ultimate review of specification, design, and code generation.
- It is not unusual for a software development organization to pay between 30 and 40 percent of total project effort on testing.
- The engineer creates a series of test cases that are intended to "defeat" the software that has been built.
- In fact, testing is the one step in the software process that could be viewed (psychologically, at least) as destructive rather than constructive.

Type of Testing Approach

- Verification and Validation approach:
- *Verification* refers to the set of activities that ensure that software correctly implements a specific function.
- *Validation* refers to a different set of activities that ensure that the software that has been built is traceable to customer requirements.
- Verification: "Are we building the product right?"
- Validation: "Are we building the right product?

Testing Strategies

- Initially, system engineering defines the role of software and leads to software requirements analysis, where the information domain, function, behavior, performance, constraints, and validation criteria for software are established.

- Moving inward along the spiral, you come to design and finally to coding. To develop computer software, you spiral inward (counterclockwise) along streamlines that decrease the level of abstraction on each turn.

Unit Testing:

- Unit is the smallest part of a software system which is testable it may include code files, classes and methods which can be tested individual for correctness.
- Unit is a process of validating such small building block of a complex system, much before testing an integrated large module or the system as a whole.
- Driver and/or stub software must be developed for each unit test a driver is nothing more than a "main program" that accepts test case data, passes such data to the component, and prints relevant results.

- Stubs serve to replace modules that are subordinate (called by) the component to be tested.
- A stub or "dummy subprogram" uses the subordinate module's interface.

Integration Testing:

- Integration is defined as a set of integration among component.
- Testing the interactions between the module and interactions with other system externally is called Integration Testing.
- Testing of integrated modules to verify combined functionality after integration.
- Integration testing addresses the issues associated with the dual problems of verification and program construction.
- Modules are typically code modules, individual applications, client and server applications on a network, etc. This type of testing is especially relevant to client/server and distributed systems.
- Types of integration testing are:

−Top-down integration
−Bottom-up integration
−Regression testing
−Smoke testing
Validation Testing

- The process of evaluating software during the development process or at the end of the development process to determine whether it

satisfies specified business requirements.
- Validation Testing ensures that the product actually meets the client's needs. It can also be defined as to demonstrate that the product fulfills its intended use when deployed on appropriate environment.
- Validation testing provides final assurance that software meets all informational, functional, behavioral, and performance requirements.
- **The alpha test** is conducted at the developer's site by a representative group of end users.
- The software is used in a natural setting with the developer "looking over the shoulder" of the users and recording errors and usage problems.
- Alpha tests are conducted in a controlled environment.

- **The beta test** is conducted at one or more end-user sites.
- Unlike alpha testing, the developer generally is not present.
- Therefore, the beta test is a "live" application of the software in an environment that cannot be controlled by the developer.

System Testing

- In system testing the software and other system elements are tested as a whole.
- To test computer software, you spiral out in a clockwise direction along streamlines that increase the scope of testing with each turn.
- System testing verifies that all elements mesh properly and that overall system function/

performance is achieved.

- **Recovery testing** is a system test that forces the software to fail in a variety of ways and verifies that recovery is properly performed.
- If recovery is automatic (performed by the system itself), re initialization, check pointing mechanisms, data recovery, and restart are evaluated for correctness. If recovery requires human intervention, the mean-time-to-repair (MTTR) is evaluated to determine whether it is within acceptable limits.
- **Security testing** attempts to verify that protection mechanisms built into a system will, in fact, protect it from improper penetration.
- During security testing, the tester plays the role(s) of the individual who desires to penetrate the system.
- **Stress testing** executes a system in a manner that demands resources in abnormal quantity, frequency, or volume.
- A variation of stress testing is a technique called sensitivity testing.
- **Performance testing** is designed to test the run-time performance of software within the context of an integrated system.
- Performance testing occurs throughout all steps in the testing process.
- Even at the unit level, the performance of an individual module may be assessed as tests are conducted.
- **Deployment testing**, sometimes called configuration testing, exercises the software in each environment in which it is to operate.

- In addition, deployment testing examines all installation procedures and specialized installation software that will be used by customers, and all documentation that will be used to introduce the software to end users.

Acceptance Testing

- Acceptance Testing is a level of the software testing where a system is tested for acceptability.
- The purpose of this test is to evaluate the system's compliance with the business requirements and assess whether it is acceptable for delivery.
- It is a formal testing with respect to user needs, requirements, and business processes conducted to determine whether or not a system satisfies the acceptance criteria and to enable the user, customers or other authorized entity to determine whether or not to accept the system.
- Acceptance Testing is performed after System Testing and before making the system available for actual use.

4. White Box Testing and Black Box Testing

White box testing

- White-box testing, sometimes called glass-box testing, is a test-case design philosophy that uses the control structure described as part of component-level design to derive test cases.

- Using white-box testing methods, you can derive test cases that

1. Guarantee that all independent paths within a module have been exercised at least once.
2. Exercise all logical decisions on their true and false sides.
3. Execute all loops at their boundaries and within their operational bounds.
4. Exercise internal data structures to ensure their validity.

- White Box Testing method is applicable to the following levels of software testing:

– It is mainly applied to Unit testing and Integration testing

–Unit Testing: For testing paths within a unit.
–Integration Testing: For testing paths between units.
–System Testing: For testing paths between subsystems.
White box testing advantages

- Testing can be commenced at an earlier stage. One need not wait for the GUI to be available.
- Testing is more thorough, with the possibility of covering most paths.

White box testing disadvantages

- Since tests can be very complex, highly skilled resources are required, with thorough knowledge of programming and implementation.

- Test script maintenance can be a burden if the implementation changes too frequently.
- Since this method of testing it closely tied with the application being testing, tools to cater to every kind of implementation/platform may not be readily available.

Black Box Testing

- Black-box testing, also called behavioral testing, focuses on the functional requirements of the software.
- That is, black-box testing techniques enable you to derive sets of input conditions that will fully exercise all functional requirements for a program.
- Black-box testing is not an alternative to white-box techniques. Rather, it is a complementary approach that is likely to uncover a different class of errors than white box methods.
- Black-box testing attempts to find errors in the following categories:

1. Incorrect or missing functions
2. Interface errors
3. Errors in data structures or external database access
4. Behavior or performance errors
5. Initialization and termination errors.

- Black Box Testing method is applicable to the following levels of software testing:

–It is mainly applied to System testing and Acceptance testing
–Integration Testing
–System Testing
–Acceptance Testing

- The higher the level, and hence the bigger and more complex the box, the more black box testing method comes into use.

Black box testing advantages

- Tests are done from a user's point of view and will help in exposing discrepancies in the specifications.
- Tester need not know programming languages or how the software has been implemented.
- Tests can be conducted by a body independent from the developers, allowing for an objective perspective and the avoidance of developer-bias.
- Test cases can be designed as soon as the specifications are complete.

Black box testing disadvantages

- Only a small number of possible inputs can be tested and many program paths will be left untested.
- Without clear specifications, which is the situation in many projects, test cases will be difficult to design.
- Tests can be redundant if the software designer/ developer has already run a test case.
- Ever wondered why a soothsayer closes the eyes when foretelling events? So is almost the case in

Black Box Testing.

5. Quality Function Deployment (QFD)

- Quality function deployment (QFD) is a quality management technique that translates the needs of the customer into technical requirements for software.
- QFD "concentrates on maximizing customer satisfaction from the software engineering process"
- To accomplish this, QFD emphasizes an understanding of what is valuable to the customer and then deploys these values throughout the engineering process.
- QFD identifies three types of requirements:

Normal requirements

- The objectives and goals that are stated for a product or system during meetings with the customer.
- If these requirements are present, the customer is satisfied. Examples of normal requirements might be requested types of graphical displays, specific system functions, and defined levels of performance.

Expected requirements

- These requirements are implicit to the product or system and may be so fundamental that the customer does not explicitly state them.
- Their absence will be a cause for significant dissatisfaction.

Exciting requirements

- These features go beyond the customer's expectations and prove to be very satisfying when present.
- For example, software for a new mobile phone comes with standard features, but is coupled with a set of unexpected capabilities that delight every user of the product.

Although QFD concepts can be applied across the entire software process, specific QFD techniques are applicable to the requirements elicitation activity.

QFD uses customer interviews and observation, surveys, and examination of historical data as raw data for the requirements gathering activity.

6. Testing Conventional Applications

Software Testing Fundamentals

The following characteristics lead to testable software.
Operability.

- "The better it works, the more efficiently it can be tested."
- If a system is designed and implemented with quality in mind, relatively few bugs will block the execution of tests, allowing testing to progress without fits and starts.

Observability.

- "What you see is what you test."
- Inputs provided as part of testing produce distinct outputs.
- System states and variables are visible or queriable during execution. Incorrect output is easily identified. Internal errors are automatically detected and reported. Source code is accessible.

Controllability.

- "The better we can control the software, the more the testing can be automated and optimized."
- All possible outputs can be generated through some combination of input, and I/O formats are consistent and structured.
- All code is executable through some combination of input. Software and hardware states and variables can be controlled directly by the test engineer.
- Tests can be conveniently specified, automated, and reproduced.

Decomposability.

- "By controlling the scope of testing, we can more quickly isolate problems and perform smarter retesting."
- The software system is built from independent modules that can be tested independently.

Simplicity.

- "The less there is to test, the more quickly we can test it."

- The program should exhibit functional simplicity (e.g., the feature set is the minimum necessary to meet requirements); structural simplicity (e.g., architecture is modularized to limit the propagation of faults), and code simplicity (e.g., a coding standard is adopted for ease of inspection and maintenance).

Stability.

- "The fewer the changes, the fewer the disruptions to testing."
- Changes to the software are infrequent, controlled when they do occur, and do not invalidate existing tests.
- The software recovers well from failures.

Understandability.

- "The more information we have, the smarter we will test."
- The architectural design and the dependencies between internal, external, and shared components are well understood.
- Technical documentation is instantly accessible, well organized, specific and detailed, and accurate. Changes to the design are communicated to testers.

7. Testing Object Oriented Applications

Unit Testing in the OO Context

- When object-oriented software is considered, the concept of the unit changes.
- Encapsulation drives the definition of classes and objects.
- This means that each class and each instance of a class (object) packages attributes (data) and the operations (also known as methods or services) that manipulate these data.
- Rather than testing an individual module, the smallest testable unit is the encapsulated class.
- Because a class can contain a number of different operations and a particular operation may exist as part of a number of different classes, the meaning of unit testing changes dramatically.
- Unlike unit testing of conventional software, which tends to focus on the algorithmic detail of a module and the data that flows across the module interface, class testing for OO software is driven by the operations encapsulated by the class and the state behavior of the class.

Integration Testing in the OO Context

- Because object-oriented software does not have a hierarchical control structure, conventional top-down and bottom-up integration strategies have little meaning.
- In addition, integrating operations one at a time into a class (the conventional incremental integration approach) is often impossible because of the "direct and indirect interactions of the components that

make up the class".

- There are two different strategies for integration testing of OO systems.
- The first, thread-based testing, integrates the set of classes required to respond to one input or event for the system. Each thread is integrated and tested individually.
- Regression testing is applied to ensure that no side effects occur.
- The second integration approach, use-based testing, begins the construction of the system by testing those classes (called independent classes) that use very few (if any) of server classes.
- After the independent classes are tested, the next layer of classes, called dependent classes, that use the independent classes are tested.
- Cluster testing is one step in the integration testing of OO software.
- Here, a cluster of collaborating classes (determined by examining the CRC and object relationship model) is exercised by designing test cases that attempt to uncover.

Validation Testing in an OO Context

- At the validation or system level, the details of class connections disappear.
- Like conventional validation, the validation of OO software focuses on user-visible actions and user-recognizable outputs from the system.

- To assist in the derivation of validation tests, the tester should draw upon use cases that are part of the requirements model.
- The use case provides a scenario that has a high likelihood of uncovered errors in user-interaction requirements.
- Conventional black-box testing methods can be used to drive validation tests.

8. Testing Web Applications

- WebApp testing is a collection of related activities with a single goal: to uncover errors in WebApp content, function, usability, navigability, performance, capacity, and security.
- To accomplish this, a testing strategy that encompasses both reviews and executable testing is applied.

Dimensions of Quality

Content is evaluated at both a syntactic and semantic level. At the syntactic level, spelling, punctuation, and grammar are assessed for text-based documents. At a semantic level, correctness (of information presented), Consistency (across the entire content object and related objects), and lack of ambiguity are all assessed.

Function is tested to uncover errors that indicate lack of conformance to customer requirements. Each WebApp function is assessed for correctness, instability, and general conformance to appropriate implementation standards (e.g., Java or AJAX language standards).

Structure is assessed to ensure that it properly delivers WebApp content and unction, that it is extensible, and that it can be supported as new content or functionality is added.

Usability is tested to ensure that each category of user is supported by the interface and can learn and apply all required navigation syntax and semantics.

Navigability is tested to ensure that all navigation syntax and semantics are exercised to uncover any navigation errors (e.g., dead links, improper links, and erroneous links).

Performance is tested under a variety of operating conditions, configurations, and loading to ensure that the system is responsive to user interaction and handles extreme loading without unacceptable operational degradation.

Compatibility is tested by executing the WebApp in a variety of different host configurations on both the client and server sides. The intent is to find errors that are specific to a unique host configuration.

Interoperability is tested to ensure that the WebApp properly interfaces with other applications and/or databases.

Security is tested by assessing potential vulnerabilities and attempting to exploit each. Any successful penetration attempt is deemed a security failure.

Content Testing

- Errors in WebApp content can be as trivial as minor typographical errors or as significant as incorrect information, improper organization, or violation of intellectual property laws.

- Content testing attempts to uncover these and many other problems before the user encounters them.
- Content testing combines both reviews and the generation of executable test cases.
- Reviews are applied to uncover semantic errors in content.
- Executable testing is used to uncover content errors that can be traced to dynamically derived content that is driven by data acquired from one or more databases.

User Interface Testing

- Verification and validation of a WebApp user interface occurs at three distinct points.
- During requirements analysis, the interface model is reviewed to ensure that it conforms to stakeholder requirements and to other elements of the requirements model.
- During design the interface design model is reviewed to ensure that generic quality criteria established for all user interfaces have been achieved and that application-specific interface design issues have been properly addressed.
- During testing, the focus shifts to the execution of application-specific aspects of user interaction as they are manifested by interface syntax and semantics.
- In addition, testing provides a final assessment of usability.

Component-Level Testing

- Component-level testing, also called function testing, focuses on a set of tests that attempt to uncover errors in WebApp functions.
- Each WebApp function is a software component (implemented in one of a variety of programming or scripting languages) and can be tested using black-box (and in some cases, white-box) techniques.
- Component-level test cases are often driven by forms-level input. Once forms data are defined, the user selects a button or other control mechanism to initiate execution.

Navigation Testing

- The job of navigation testing is to ensure that the mechanisms that allow the WebApp user to travel through the WebApp are all functional and to validate that each navigation semantic unit (NSU) can be achieved by the appropriate user category.
- Navigation mechanisms should be tested are Navigation links, Redirects, Bookmarks, Frames and framesets, Site maps, Internal search engines.

Configuration Testing

- Configuration variability and instability are important factors that make WebApp testing a challenge. Hardware, operating system(s), browsers, storage capacity, network communication speeds, and a variety of other client-side factors are difficult to predict for each user.
- One user's impression of the WebApp and the manner in which she interacts with it can differ significantly from another user's experience, if both users are not working within the same client-side configuration.
- The job of configuration testing is not to exercise every possible client-side configuration.
- Rather, it is to test a set of probable client-side and server-side configurations to ensure that the user experience will be the same on all of them and to isolate errors that may be specific to a particular configuration.

Security Testing

- Security tests are designed to probe vulnerabilities of the client-side environment, the network communications that occur as data are passed from client to server and back again, and the server-side environment.
- Each of these domains can be attacked, and it is the job of the security tester to uncover weaknesses that can be exploited by those with the intent to do so.

Performance Testing

- Performance testing is used to uncover performance problems that can result from lack of server-side resources, inappropriate network bandwidth, inadequate database capabilities, faulty or weak operating system capabilities, poorly designed WebApp functionality, and other hardware or software issues that can lead to degraded client-server performance.

9. Verification and Validation

Verification

1. Verification is a static practice of verifying documents, design, code and program.

2. It does not involve executing the code.

3. It is human based checking of documents and files.

4. Verification uses methods like inspections, reviews, walkthroughs, and Desk-checking etc.

5. Verification is to check whether the software conforms to specifications.

6. It can catch errors that validation cannot catch. It is low level exercise.

7. Target is requirements specification, application and software architecture, high level, complete

design, and database design etc.

8. Verification is done by QA team to ensure that the software is as per the specifications in the

SRS document.

9. It generally comes first-done before validation.

Validation

1. Validation is a dynamic mechanism of validating and testing the actual product.

2. It always involves executing the code.

3. It is computer based execution of program.

4. Validation uses methods like black box (functional) testing, gray box testing, and white

box (structural) testing etc.

5. Validation is to check whether software meets the customer expectations and requirements.

6. It can catch errors that verification cannot catch. It is High Level Exercise.

7. Target is actual product-a unit, a module, a bent of integrated modules, and effective final product.

8. Validation is carried out with the involvement of testing team.

9. It generally follows after verification.

Software Coding & Testing-II

1. **Software Quality Assurance (SQA)**

- Software quality assurance (often called quality management) is an umbrella activity that is applied throughout the software process.
- It is planned and systematic pattern of activities necessary to provide high degree of confidence in the quality of a product.
- Software quality assurance (SQA) encompasses

–An SQA process.

–Specific quality assurance and quality control tasks.

–Effective software engineering practice.

–Control of all software work products and the changes made to them.

– A procedure to ensure compliance with software development standards.

–Measurement and reporting mechanisms.

Importance of SQA

- Quality control and assurance are essential activities for any business that produces products to be used by others.
- Prior to the twentieth century, quality control was the sole responsibility of the craftsperson who built a product.
- As time passed and mass production techniques became commonplace, quality control became an activity performed by people other than the ones who built the product.
- Software quality is one of the pivotal aspects of a software development company.
- Software quality assurance starts from the beginning of a project, right from the analysis phase.
- SQA checks the adherence to software product standards, processes, and procedures.
- SQA includes the systematic process of assuring that standards and procedures are established and are followed throughout the software development life cycle and test cycle as well.
- The compliance of the built with agreed-upon standards and procedures is evaluated through process monitoring, product evaluation, project management etc.
- The major reason of involving software quality assurance in the process of software product development is to make sure that the final product built is as per the requirement specification and comply with the standards.

SQA Activities

Prepare an SQA plan for a project

- The plan is developed as part of project planning and is reviewed by all stakeholders.
- Quality assurance actions performed by the software engineering team and the SQA group are governed by the plan.
- The plan identifies evaluations to be performed, audits and reviews to be conducted, standards that are applicable to the project, procedures for error reporting and tracking, work products that are produced by the SQA group, and feedback that will be provided to the software team.

Participate in the development of the project's software process description

- The software team selects a process for the work to be performed.
- The SQA group reviews the process description for compliance with organizational policy, internal software standards, externally imposed standards, and other parts of the software project plan.

Review software engineering activities to verify compliance with the defined software process.

- The SQA group identifies, documents, and tracks deviations from the process and verifies that corrections have been made.

Audit designated software work products to verify compliance with those defined as part of the software process

- The SQA group reviews selected work products; identifies, documents, and tracks deviations; verifies that corrections have been made; and periodically reports the results of its work to the project manager.

Ensure that deviations in software work and work products are documented and handled according to a documented procedure.

- Deviations may be encountered in the project plan, process description, applicable standards, or software engineering work products.

Records any noncompliance and reports to senior management

- Noncompliance items are tracked until they are resolved.

SQA Techniques

Data Collection

Statistical quality assurance implies the following steps:

1. Information about software defects is collected and categorized.
2. An attempt is made to trace each defect to its underlying cause (e.g., non- conformance to specifications, design error, violation of standards, poor communication with

the customer).

3. Using the Pareto principle (80 percent of the defects can be traced to 20 per- cent of all possible causes), isolate the 20 percent (the "vital few").

4. Once the vital few causes have been identified, move to correct the problems that have caused the defects.

-   A software engineering organization collects information on defects for a period of one year.
-   Some of the defects are uncovered as software is being developed.
-   Others are encountered after the software has been released to its end-users. Although hundreds of different errors are uncovered, all can be tracked to one (or more) of the following causes:

–incomplete or erroneous specifications (IES)

–misinterpretation of customer communication (MCC)

–intentional deviation from specifications (IDS)

–violation of programming standards (VPS)

–error in data representation (EDR)

–inconsistent component interface (ICI)

–error in design logic (EDL)

–incomplete or erroneous testing (IET)

–inaccurate or incomplete documentation (IID)

–error in programming language translation of design (PLT)

–ambiguous or inconsistent human/computer interface (HCI)

–miscellaneous (MIS)

Six Sigma: Refer Section 4 SQA standards

1. Software Reviews (Formal Technical Reviews)

A formal technical review (FTR) is a software quality control activity performed by software engineers (and others).

The objectives of an FTR are:

1. To uncover errors in function, logic, or implementation for any representation of the software.
2. To verify that the software under review meets its requirements.
3. To ensure that the software has been represented according to predefined standards.
4. To achieve software that is developed in a uniform manner.
5. To make projects more manageable.

Review Reporting and Record Keeping

- During the FTR, a reviewer (the recorder) actively records all issues that have been raised.
- These are summarized at the end of the review meeting, and a review issues list is produced. In addition, a formal technical review summary report is completed.

Review Guidelines

- Guidelines for conducting formal technical reviews must be established in advance, distributed to all reviewers, agreed upon, and then followed.
- A review that is un-controlled can often be worse than no review at all.

- Review the product, not the producer.
- Set an agenda and maintain it.
- Limit debate and denial:
- Speak problem areas, but don't attempt to solve every problem noted.
- Take written notes.
- Limit the number of participants and insist upon advance preparation.
- Develop a checklist for each product that is likely to be reviewed.
- Allocate resources and schedule time for FTRs
- Conduct meaningful training for all reviewers.
- Review your early reviews.

Sample-Driven Reviews

- In an ideal setting, every software engineering work product would undergo a formal technical review.
- In the real word of software projects, resources are limited and time is short.
- As a consequence, reviews are often skipped, even though their value as a quality control mechanism is recognized.

3. Software Reliability

- Software reliability is defined in statistical terms as "the probability of failure-free operation of a computer program in a specified environment for a specified time".

Measures of Reliability

- A simple measure of reliability is meantime-between-failure (**MTBF**):

  - MTBF = MTTF + MTTR

- Where the acronyms MTTF and MTTR are mean-time-to-failure and mean-time-to- repair, respectively.
- Many researchers argue that MTBF is a far more useful measure than other quality-related software metrics. An end user is concerned with failures, not with the total defect count.
- Because each defect contained within a program does not have the same failure rate, the total defect count provides little indication of the reliability of a system.
- An alternative measure of reliability is failures-in-time (FIT) a statistical measure of how many failures a component will have over one billion hours of operation.

Software Safety

- Software safety is a software quality assurance activity that focuses on the identification and assessment of potential hazards that may affect software negatively and cause an entire system to fail.

- If hazards can be identified early in the software process, software design features can be specified that will either eliminate or control potential hazards.
- A modeling and analysis process is conducted as part of software safety.
- Initially, hazards are identified and categorized by criticality and risk.
- Although software reliability and software safety are closely related to one another, it is important to understand the subtle difference between them.
- Software reliability uses statistical analysis to determine the likelihood that a software failure will occur.
- However, the occurrence of a failure does not necessarily result in a hazard or accident.
- Software safety examines the ways in which failures result in conditions that can lead to an accident.

4. The quality standards ISO 9000 and 9001, Six Sigma, CMM

ISO 9001

- In order to bring quality in product & service, many organizations are adopting Quality Assurance System.
- ISO standards are issued by the International Organization for Standardization (ISO) in Switzerland.

- Proper documentation is an important part of an ISO 9001 Quality Management System.
- ISO 9001 is the quality assurance standard that applies to software engineering.
- It includes, requirements that must be present for an effective quality assurance system.
- ISO 9001 standard is applicable to all engineering discipline.
- The requirements delineated by ISO 9001:2000 address topics such as

–Management responsibility
–quality system
–contract review
–design control
–document
–data control
–product identification
–Traceability
–process control
–inspection
–Testing
–preventive action
–control of quality records
–internal quality
–Audits
–Training
–Servicing

- Statistical techniques.

- In order for a software organization to become registered to ISO 9001:2000, it must establish policies and procedures to address each of the requirements just noted (and others) and then be able to demonstrate that these policies and procedures are being followed.

Six Sigma

- Six sigma is "A generic quantitative approach to improvement that applies to any process."
- "Six Sigma is a disciplined, data-driven approach and methodology for eliminating in any process from manufacturing to transactional and from product to service."
- To achieve six sigma a process must not produce more than 3.4 defects per million opportunities.
- 5 Sigma -> 230 defects per million
- 4 Sigma -> 6210 defects per million
- Six sigma have two methodologies

1. DMAIC (Define, Measure, Analyze, Improve, Control)

–Define: Define the problem or process to improve upon related to the customer and goals

– Measure: How can you measure this process in a systematic way?

–Analyze: Analyze the process or problem and identify the way in which it can be improved.

What are the root causes of problems within the process?

–Improve: Once you know the causes of the problems, present solutions for them and implement them

– Control: Utilize Statistical Process Control to continuously measure your results and ensure you are improving

– Several Software Packages available to assist in measuring yield, defects per million opportunities, etc.

2. DMADV: (Define, Measure, Analyze, Design, Verify)

– Define, Measure and analyze are similar to above method.

– Design: Avoid root causes of defects and meet the customer requirements.

–Verify: To verify the process, compare the process with the standard plan and find differences.

CMM (Capability Maturity Model)

- To determine an organization's current state of process maturity, the SEI uses an assessment that results in a five point grading scheme.
- The grading scheme determines compliance with a capability maturity model (CMM) that defines key activities required at different levels of process maturity.
- The SEI approach provides a measure of the global effectiveness of a company's software engineering practices and establishes five process maturity levels

that are defined in the following manner:

- **Level 1: Initial.** The software process is characterized as ad hoc and occasionally even chaotic. Few processes are defined, and success depends on individual effort.
- **Level 2: Repeatable.** Basic project management processes are established to track cost, schedule, and functionality. The necessary process discipline is in place to repeat earlier successes on projects with similar applications.
- **Level 3: Defined.** The software process for both management and engineering activities is documented, standardized, and integrated into an organization wide software process. All projects use a documented and approved version of the organization's process for developing and supporting software. This level includes all characteristics defined for level 2.
- **Level 4: Managed.** Detailed measures of the software process and product quality are collected. Both the software process and products are quantitatively understood and controlled using detailed measures. This level includes all characteristics defined for level 3.
- **Level 5: Optimizing.** Continuous process improvement is enabled by quantitative feedback from the process and from testing innovative ideas and technologies. This level includes all characteristics defined for level 4.

5. SQA Plan

The SQA Plan provides a road map for instituting software quality assurance.

Developed by the SQA group (or by the software team if an SQA group does not exist), the plan serves as a template for SQA activities that are instituted for each software project.

The standard recommends a structure that identifies:

1. The purpose and scope of the plan.
2. A description of all software engineering work products (e.g., models, documents, source code) that fall within the purview of SQA.
3. All applicable standards and practices that are applied during the software process.
4. SQA actions and tasks (including reviews and audits) and their placement throughout the software process.
5. The tools and methods that support SQA actions and tasks.
6. Software configuration management procedures.
7. Methods for assembling, safeguarding, and maintaining all SQA-related records.
8. Organizational roles and responsibilities relative to product quality.

CHAPTER EIGHT

Software Maintenance and Configuration Management

1. Types of Software Maintenance

- In a software lifetime, type of maintenance may vary based on its nature. It may be just a routine maintenance tasks as some bug discovered by some user or it may be a large event in itself based on maintenance size or nature. Following are some types of maintenance based on their characteristics:

Corrective Maintenance:

- This includes modifications and updations done in order to correct or fix problems, which are either discovered by user or concluded by user error reports.
- Corrective maintenance deals with the repair of faults or defects found in day-today system

functions.

- A defect can result due to errors in software design, logic and coding.
- Design errors occur when changes made to the software are incorrect, incomplete, wrongly communicated, or the change request is misunderstood.

Adaptive Maintenance:

- This includes modifications and updations applied to keep the software product up-to date and tuned to the ever changing world of technology and business environment.
- Adaptive maintenance is the implementation of changes in a part of the system, which has been affected by a change that occurred in some other part of the system.
- Adaptive maintenance consists of adapting software to changes in the environment such as the hardware or the operating system.
- The term environment in this context refers to the conditions and the influences which act (from outside) on the system.

Perfective Maintenance:

- This includes modifications and updates done in order to keep the software usable over long period of time. It includes new features, new user requirements for refining the software and improve its reliability and performance.

- Perfective maintenance mainly deals with implementing new or changed user requirements.
- Perfective maintenance involves making functional enhancements to the system in addition to the activities to increase the system's performance even when the changes have not been suggested by faults.
- This includes enhancing both the function and efficiency of the code and changing the functionalities of the system as per the users' changing needs.

Preventive Maintenance:

- This includes modifications and updations to prevent future problems of the software. It aims to attend problems, which are not significant at this moment but may cause serious issues in future.
- Preventive maintenance involves performing activities to prevent the occurrence of errors.
- It tends to reduce the software complexity thereby improving program understandability and increasing software maintainability. It comprises documentation updating, code optimization, and code restructuring.
- Documentation updating involves modifying the documents affected by the changes in order to correspond to the present state of the system.

2. Re-Engineering

- When we need to update the software to keep it to the current market, without impacting its functionality, it is called software re-engineering.

- It is a thorough process where the design of software is changed and programs are re-written.
- Legacy software cannot keep tuning with the latest technology available in the market.
- As the hardware become obsolete, updating of software becomes a headache.
- Even if software grows old with time, its functionality does not.
- For example, initially UNIX was developed in assembly language. When language C came into existence, UNIX was re-engineered in C, because working in assembly language was difficult.

- Other than this, sometimes programmers notice that few parts of software need more maintenance than others and they also need re-engineering.

Re-Engineering Process

- **Decide** what to re-engineer. Is it whole software or a part of it?
- **Perform** Reverse Engineering, in order to obtain specifications of existing software.
- **Restructure** Program if required. For example, changing function-oriented programs into object-oriented programs. Re-structure data as required.
- **Apply** Forward engineering concepts in order to get re-engineered software.

2. Reverse Engineering

- Reverse engineering can extract design information from source code, but the abstraction level, the completeness of the documentation, the degree to which tools and a human analyst work together, and the

- Directionality of the process are highly variable.
- The *abstraction* level of a reverse engineering process and the tools used to effect it refers to the sophistication of the design information that can be extracted from source code.
- Ideally, the abstraction level should be as high as possible.
- That is, the reverse engineering process should be capable of deriving procedural design representations (a low-level abstraction), program and data structure information (a somewhat higher level of abstraction), object models, data and/or control flow models (a relatively high level of abstraction), and entity relationship models (a high level of abstraction).
- As the abstraction level increases, you are provided with information that will allow easier understanding of the program.
- The *completeness* of a reverse engineering process refers to the level of detail that is provided at an abstraction level. In most cases, the completeness decreases as the abstraction level increases.
- *Interactivity* refers to the degree to which the human is "integrated" with automated tools to create an effective reverse engineering process.
- In most cases, as the abstraction level increases, interactivity must increase or completeness will suffer.
- The *directionality* of the reverse engineering process is one-way, all information extracted from the source

code is provided to the software engineer who can then use it during any maintenance activity.

3. Forward Engineering

- Forward engineering is a process of obtaining desired software from the specifications in hand which were brought down by means of reverse engineering. It assumes that there was some software engineering already done in the past.
- Forward engineering is same as software engineering process with only one difference it is carried out always after reverse engineering.
- The forward engineering process applies software engineering principles, concepts, and methods to re-create an existing application. In most cases, forward engineering does not simply create a modern equivalent of an older program.
- Rather, new user and technology requirements are integrated into the reengineering effort.
- The redeveloped program extends the capabilities of the older application.

4. The SCM (Software Configuration Management) Process

- The software configuration management process defines a series of tasks that have four primary objectives:

1. To identify all items that collectively define the software configuration.
2. To manage changes to one or more of these items.

3. To facilitate the construction of different versions of an application.
4. To ensure that software quality is maintained as the configuration evolves over time.

- Referring to the figure, SCM tasks can viewed as concentric layers.

- SCIs (Software Configuration Item) flow outward through these layers throughout their useful life, ultimately becoming part of the software configuration of one or more versions of an application or system.
- As an SCI moves through a layer, the actions implied by each SCM task may or may not be applicable. For example, when a new SCI is created, it must be identified.
- However, if no changes are requested for the SCI, the change control layer does not apply. The SCI is assigned to a specific version of the software (version control mechanisms come into play).
- A record of the SCI (its name, creation date, version designation, etc.) is maintained for configuration auditing purposes and reported to those with a need to know.

•

In the sections that follow, we examine each of these SCM process layers in more detail.

Figure: Layers of SCM Process

6. Identification of Objects in the Software Configuration

- To control and manage software configuration items, each should be separately named and then organized using an object-oriented approach.
- Two types of objects can be identified: basic objects and aggregate objects.
- **A basic object** is a unit of information that you create during analysis, design, code, or test.
- For example, a basic object might be a section of a requirements specification, part of a design model,

source code for a component, or a suite of test cases that are used to exercise the code.

- **An aggregate object** is a collection of basic objects and other aggregate objects.
- For example, a Design Specification is an aggregate object. Conceptually, it can be viewed as a named (identified) list of pointers that specify aggregate objects such as Architectural Model and Data Model, and basic objects such as Component and UML Class Diagram.
- Each object has a set of distinct features that identify it uniquely: a name, a description, a list of resources, and a "realization."
- The object name is a character string that identifies the object unambiguously.
- The object description is a list of data items that identify the SCI type (e.g., model element, program, data) represented by the object, a project identifier, and change and/or version information.
- Resources are "entities that are provided, processed, referenced or otherwise required by the object".

7. Version Control and Change Control

Version Control

- Version control combines procedures and tools to manage different versions of configuration objects that are created during the software process.
- A version control system implements or is directly integrated with four major capabilities:

1. A project database (repository) that stores all relevant configuration objects.
2. A version management capability that stores all versions of a configuration object.
3. A make facility that enables you to collect all relevant configuration objects and construct a specific version of the software.

- In addition, version control and change control systems often implement an issues tracking capability that enables the team to record and track the status of all outstanding issues associated with each configuration object.
- A number of version control systems establish a change set—a collection of all changes (to some baseline configuration) that are required to create a specific version of the software.
- A change set "captures all changes to all files in the configuration along with the reason for changes and details of who made the changes and when."
- A number of named change sets can be identified for an application or system.
- This enables you to construct a version of the software by specifying the change sets (by name) that must be applied to the baseline configuration.
- To accomplish this, a system modeling approach is applied. The system model contains:

1. A template that includes a component hierarchy and a "build order" for the components that describes how the system must be constructed.
2. Construction rules.
3. Verification rules.

- The primary difference in approaches is the sophistication of the attributes that are used to construct specific versions and variants of a system and the mechanics of the process for construction.

Change Control

- For a large software project, uncontrolled change rapidly leads to chaos.
- For such projects, change control combines human procedures and automated tools to provide a mechanism for the control of change.
- A change request is submitted and evaluated to assess technical merit, potential side effects, overall impact on other configuration objects and system functions, and the projected cost of the change.
- The results of the evaluation are presented as a change report, which is used by a change control authority
- (CCA)—a person or group that makes a final decision on the status and priority of the change.
- An engineering change order (ECO) is generated for each approved change.
- The ECO describes the change to be made, the constraints that must be respected, and the criteria for review and audit.

CHAPTER NINE

Software Engineering and Software as a Service

1. Software as a Service

*   SaaS, or Software as a Service, describes any cloud service where consumers are able to access software applications over the internet.
*   Google, Twitter, Facebook and Flickr are all examples of SaaS, with users able to access the services via any internet enabled device.
*   Enterprise users are able to use applications for a range of needs, including accounting and invoicing, tracking sales, planning, performance monitoring and communications.
*   SaaS is often referred to as software-on-demand and utilizing it is akin to renting software rather than buying it.
*   With traditional software applications you would purchase the software upfront as a package and then

install it onto your computer.

- The software's license may also limit the number of users and/or devices where the software can be deployed.
- Software as a Service users, however, subscribe to the software rather than purchase it, usually on a monthly basis.
- Applications are purchased and used online with files saved in the cloud rather than on individual computers.
- There are a number of reasons why SaaS is beneficial to organizations and personal users alike:

– No additional hardware costs; the processing power required to run the applications is supplied by the cloud provider.

–No initial setup costs; applications are ready to use once the user subscribes.

– Pay for what you use; if a piece of software is only needed for a limited period then it is only paid for over that period and subscriptions can usually be halted at any time.

– Usage is scalable; if a user decides they need more storage or additional services, for example, then they can access these on demand without needing to install new software or hardware.

–Updates are automated; whenever there is an update it is available online to existing customers, often free of charge. No new software will be required as it often is with other types of applications and the updates will usually be deployed automatically by the cloud provider.

– Cross device compatibility; SaaS applications can be accessed via any internet enabled device, which makes it ideal for those who use a number of different devices, such as internet enabled phones and tablets, and those who don't always use the same computer.

– Accessible from any location; rather than being restricted to installations on individual computers, an application can be accessed from anywhere with an internet enabled device.

– Applications can be customized and white labelled; with some software, customization is available meaning it can be altered to suit the needs and branding of a particular customer.

- Office software is the best example of businesses utilizing SaaS. Tasks related to accounting, invoicing, sales and planning can all be performed through Software as a Service.
- Businesses may wish to use one piece of software that performs all of these tasks or several that each perform different tasks.
- The required software can be subscribed to via the internet and then accessed online via any computer in the office using a username and password.
- If needs change they can easily switch to software that better meets their requirements. Everyone who needs access to a particular piece of software can be set up as a user, whether it is one or two people or every employee in a corporation that employs hundreds.

Summary

- There are no setup costs with SaaS, as there often are with other applications.
- SaaS is scalable with upgrades available on demand.
- Access to Software as a Service is compatible across all internet enabled devices.
- As long as there is an internet connection, applications are accessible from any location.

1. SaaS Architecture.

- Application Service Providers (ASPs) basically allowed their customers to download software applications and the installation process was similar to the traditional CD-based software.
- Even though the ASP service model provided a relatively efficient means of getting software applications to the customer, it suffered a number of problems.
- The main one being the size of the actual download file, which could run into hundreds of MB; and the subsequent maintenance updates which also had to be downloaded on a regular basis.
- Without these updates the software vendors could not always ensure that their customers were running the latest version of their software.

Figure: SaaS Model

- To get around the shortfalls in the ASP, and for that matter the traditional software delivery models, a new method of delivering software was conceived.
- This new service model, Software as a Service, which was built on the core building blocks of ASP, was architected from the ground up to operate as a fully "hosted" solution.
- The diagram above illustrates the key differences between the traditional software delivery model and a SaaS-based delivery model.
- In essence, all users of SaaS-based applications run exactly the same code with customizations and configurations stored as metadata parameters.
- The key difference between SaaS and traditional software delivery is that SaaS-based applications are fully hosted within some form of data Centre environment.

- All updates to the SaaS application are carried out within the data Centre and therefore the user can always be assured that they are using the most recent version of the application.
- These applications are designed from the ground up to work and take advantage of operating within a web browser-based environment.
- Since nearly every PC comes supplied with a browser as part of the operating environment, there is hardly any implementation work required by a company's IT department.
- This allows the IT department to focus on other activities reducing support costs, and allowing a certain level of autonomy within some of the company's business units.
- SaaS is traditionally sold on a subscription basis that includes upgrades, maintenance and some level of basic support.
- These subscriptions operate on a monthly, quarterly or yearly basis, and are ideal for companies who would be using the application periodically.

3. Product Lifetime: Independent Product vs. Continuous Improvement

- In order to understand the engineering process for the software, it is essential to contrast software and hardware engineering with respect to product lifetime.
- The concept product life time concerns the life of product in the market with respect to business or commercial cost and sales measures.

- The time period of product life cycle and the length of each stage varies from product to product.
- Life cycle of one product can be over in few months, and of another product may last for many years.
- The product life cycle proceeds through multiple phases, involves many professional disciplines and requires many skills, tools and processes.
- There are three assumptions made for product lifetime:

1. Products have a limited life and thus every product has a life cycle.
2. Product sales pass through distinct stages, each posing different challenges, opportunities and problems to the seller.
3. Products require different marketing, financing, manufacturing, purchasing and human resource strategies throughout its lifetime.

- Product life time is an important factor for the difference between hardware and software.
- There are two important approaches for product lifetime (1) Independent Product, (2) Continuous Improvement.
- Quality Management (QM) is an approach to doing business that maximizes the competitiveness of an organization through continuous improvement of its products, services, people, processes, and environments.
- The continuous improvement tasks are:

–Review product, processes and practices periodically to look for rooms for improvement and efficiency enhancement.

–Conduct frequent retrospectives and experiments to continually improve team processes and effectiveness.

– Gather feedback from stakeholders on product increments and demonstrations to enhance value delivery.

–Develop a team of generalizing specialists by providing learning and practicing opportunities.

–Perform value stream analysis on existing processes to remove wastes and improve efficiency.

–Disseminate knowledge gained during carrying out the project works to the whole organization for organizational improvement.

CHAPTER TEN

Advanced Topics in SoftwareEngineering

1. Computer-Aided Software Engineering (CASE)

- Computer-aided software engineering (CASE) tools assist software engineering managers and practitioners in every activity associated with the software process.
- They automate project management activities, manage all work products produced throughout the process, and assist engineers in their analysis, design, coding and test work.
- CASE tools can be integrated within a sophisticated environment. CASE provides the software engineer with the ability to automate manual activities and to improve engineering insight.

CASE Tools Building Blocks

-
  > The *environment architecture*, composed of the hardware platform and system support (including networking software, database management, and object management services), lays the ground work for CASE. But the CASE environment itself demands other building blocks.

- A set of *portability services* provides a bridge between CASE tools and their integration framework and the environment architecture.

- The *integration framework* is a collection of specialized programs that enables individual CASE tools to communicate with one another, to create a project database, and to exhibit the same look and feel to the end-user.

- Portability services allow CASE tools and their integration framework to migrate across different *hardware platforms and operating systems* without significant adaptive maintenance.

- The building blocks depicted in Figure represent a comprehensive foundation for the integration of CASE tools. However, most CASE tools in use today have not been constructed using all these building blocks.
- In fact, some CASE tools remain "point solutions." That is, a tool is used to assist in a particular software engineering activity (e.g., analysis modeling) but does not directly communicate with other tools, is not tied into a project database, is not part of an integrated CASE environment (I- CASE).
- Although this situation is not ideal, a CASE tool can be used quite effectively, even if it is a point solution.

A taxonomy of case tools

- CASE tools can be classified by function, by their role as instruments for managers or technical people, by their use in the various steps of the software engineering process, by the environment architecture (hardware and software) that supports them, or even by their origin or cost.
- The taxonomy presented here uses function as a primary criterion.

Business process engineering tools
Analysis and design tools
Process modeling and management tools

PRO/SIM (prototyping and simulation) tools
Project planning tools
Interface design and development tools
Risk analysis tools
Prototyping tools
Project management tools
Programming tools
Requirements tracing tools
Web development tools
Metrics and management tools
Integration and testing tools
Documentation tools
Static analysis tools
System software tools
Dynamic analysis tools
Quality assurance tools
Test management tools
Database management tools
Client/server testing tools
Software configuration management tools
Reengineering tools

1. Component-Based Software Engineering

- Component-based software engineering (CBSE) is a process that emphasizes the design and construction of computer-based systems using reusable software "components."
- CBSE seems quite similar to conventional or object-oriented software engineering.
- The process begins when a software team establishes requirements for the system to be built using conventional requirements elicitation

techniques.

Activities

- **Component qualification.** System requirements and architecture define the components that will be required. Reusable components (whether COTS or in-house) are normally identified by the characteristics of their interfaces.
- **Component adaptation.** Software architecture represents design patterns that are composed of components (units of functionality), connections, and coordination.
- In essence the architecture defines the design rules for all components, identifying modes of connection and coordination.
- **Component composition.** Architectural style again plays a key role in the way in which software components are integrated to form a working system.
- **Component update.** When systems are implemented with COTS components, update is complicated by the imposition of a third party (i.e., the organization that developed the reusable component may be outside the Immediate control of the software engineering organization).

Various Components

- **Component**—a nontrivial, nearly independent, and replaceable part of a system that fulfills a clear function in the context of a well-defined architecture.
- **Run-time software component**—a dynamic bindable package of one or more programs managed as a unit and accessed through documented interfaces that can be discovered in run time.
- **Software component**—a unit of composition with contractually specified and explicit context dependencies only.
- **Business component**—the software implementation of an "autonomous" business concept or business process.
- **Qualified components**—assessed by software engineers to ensure that not only functionality, but performance, reliability, usability, and other quality factors follow to the requirements of the system or product to be built.
- **Adapted components**—adapted to modify (also called mask or wrap) unwanted or undesirable characteristics.
- **Assembled components**—integrated into an architectural style and interconnected with an appropriate infrastructure that allows the components to be coordinated and managed effectively.
- **Updated components**—replacing existing software as new versions of components become available.

3. Client/Server Software Engineering

- There are different software process models were introduced.
- Although any of them could be adapted for use during the development of software for c/s systems, two approaches are most commonly used:

- An evolutionary paradigm that makes use of event-based and/or object-oriented software engineering.
- Component based software engineering that draws on a library of COTS and in-house software components.

  - Client/server systems are developed using the classic software engineering activities analysis, design, construction, and testing—as the system evolves from a set of general business requirements to a collection of validated software components that have been implemented on client and server machines.

Software Components for Client/Server Systems

  - Instead of viewing software as a monolithic application to be implemented on one machine, the software that is appropriate for a c/s architecture has several distinct subsystems that can be allocated to the client, the server, or distributed between both machines:

- **User interaction/presentation subsystem.** This subsystem implements all functions that are typically associated with a graphical user interface.
- **Application subsystem.** This subsystem implements the requirements defined by the application within the context of the domain in which the application operates.
- **Database management subsystem.** This subsystem performs the data manipulation and management required by an application. Data manipulation and management may be as simple as the transfer of a record or as complex as the processing of sophisticated SQL transactions.

Structure of Client /Server System

Figure: Client/Server Architecture

- **File servers.** The client requests specific records from a file. The server transmits these records to the client across the network.
- **Database servers.** The client sends structured query language (SQL) requests to the server. These are transmitted as messages across the network. The server processes the SQL request and finds the requested information, passing back the results only to the client.
- **Transaction servers.** The client sends a request that invokes remote procedures at the server site. The remote procedures are a set of SQL statements.
- A transaction occurs when a request results in the execution of the remote procedure with the result transmitted back to the client.
- **Groupware servers.** When the server provides a set of applications that enable communication among clients (and the people using them) using text, images, bulletin boards, video, and other representations, a groupware architecture exists.

4. Web Engineering

- Web engineering is the process used to create high-quality Web Apps.
- Web engineering is not a perfect clone of software engineering, but it borrows many of software engineering's
- Fundamental concepts and principles, emphasizing the same technical and management activities.

- Web Engineering (WebE) is concerned with the establishment and use of sound scientific, engineering, and management principles and disciplined and systematic approaches to the successful development, deployment, and maintenance of high quality Web-based systems and applications.

Web Engineering Process

- The characteristics of Web-based systems and applications have a profound influence on the WebE process.
- Immediacy and continuous evolution dictate an iterative, incremental process model that produces WebApp releases in rapid fire sequence.
- The network-intensive nature of applications in this domain suggests a population of users that is diverse (thereby making special demands on requirements elicitation and modeling) and an application architecture that can be highly specialized (thereby making demands on design).
- Because WebApps are often content driven with an emphasis on aesthetics, it is likely that parallel development activities will be scheduled within the WebE process and involve a team of both technical and non-technical people (e.g., copywriters, graphic designers).

Frame work for Web Engineering

- As WebApps evolve from static, content-directed information sources to dynamic, user-directed application environments, the need to apply solid management and engineering principles grows in importance.
- To accomplish this, it is necessary to develop a WebE framework that encompasses an effective process model, populated by framework activities and engineering tasks.

A process model for WebE is suggested in Figure.

Figure: The WebE Process Model

- The WebE process begins with a *formulation*—an activity that identifies the goals and objectives of the WebApp and establishes the scope for the first increment.
- *Planning* estimates overall project cost, evaluates risks associated with the development effort, and defines a finely granulated development schedule for the initial WebApp increment, with a more coarsely granulated schedule for subsequent increments.
- *Analysis* establishes technical requirements for the WebApp and identifies the content items that will be incorporated.
- Requirements for graphic design (aesthetics) are also defined.
- The *engineering* activity incorporates two parallel tasks illustrated on the right side of Figure. *Content design and production* are tasks performed by nontechnical members of the WebE team.

- The intent of these tasks is to design, produce, and/or acquire all text, graphics, audio, and video content that are to become integrated into the WebApp.
- *Page generation* is a construction activity that makes heavy use of automated tools for WebApp creation.
- *Testing* exercises WebApp navigation; attempts to uncover errors in applets, scripts, and forms; and

helps ensure that the WebApp will operate correctly in different environments (e.g., with different browsers).

- Each increment produced as part of the WebE process is reviewed during *customer evaluation.*
- This is the point at which changes are requested (scope extensions occur).

MR. RAHUL SHARMA
Asst. Prof.(CSE)
Parul Institute of Technology,
Parul University
Vadodara , Gujarat

MR. RAHUL ANJANA
Asst. Prof.(CSE)
Parul Institute of Technology,
Parul University
Vadodara , Gujarat

MS. MONIKA VERMA
Asst. Prof.(CSE)
Prestige Institute of Engineering Managment
and Research, Indore, M.P.

9 798888 749 1387